Where
the
heart
is

Karen Martini

Where the heart is

Photography by Petrina Tinslay

LANTERN

an imprint of

PENGUIN BOOKS

Contents

Ingredients

When you see these ingredients in my recipes, unless it says otherwise, I recommend you use the following:

> freshly ground black pepper from a pepper grinder, or black peppercorns pounded to medium grounds in a mortar and pestle

> salt flakes – I use the fantastic delicate pink Murray River salt flakes, which are available at gourmet shops and delis

> for salt to add to boiling water, use coarsely ground sea salt or rock salt

> milk – I use full-fat milk

> thickened cream – 35% fat

> pure cream – 45% fat

> butter – unsalted

> eggs – free-range

> sugar – castor sugar

> oil – extra virgin olive oil in almost every case

> any chicken or pork – free-range or organic

> gelatine – gelatine sheets, not powder. I use Alba gold leaf or Gelita gold leaf; both products weigh 10 g for 6 sheets.

> shallots – these are the small-bulbed brown (or sometimes purple/pink) onions with crackling skin. They are milder and sweeter than normal onions.

> spring onions – are also known as green onions, and as shallots in NSW. These graduate from white at the bottom to green at the top.

rough quantity guidelines

1 lemon, juiced = 125 ml

1 egg = 55–60 g

1 large potato = 180 g

1 bunch herbs = 1½ cups

1 cup dried beans = 160 g

1 brown onion = 130 g

Introduction

If I followed road maps in the same way I follow recipes, I'm sure that I would constantly end up in entirely unexpected places. And if I drove the same way I cook, I'm equally sure that I would usually be delighted wherever I arrived. Perhaps the next time I would take a shorter route, or a more scenic one, but in most cases I would return. Sometimes, of course, I would not go back, but experience is never wasted.

So for me, as an intuitive cook, documenting my food seemed a special challenge. Over the years, of course, I had to have formal recipes for my restaurant kitchens, but so much of my food is created at home that, although these creations are echoed and refined in the restaurant, it is the spirit and style of home-cooking that I wish to share in this book.

The task of collating and synthesising twenty years of professional and personal experience was not an easy one, but it was exciting and made me reflect on my past. My recipes were sometimes typed, often handwritten and frequently scrawled on endless sheets of paper, on the back of old menus, gas bills, invoices and business cards. They reflected times shared with family and friends, at home and on holiday, barbecues, raucous parties, romantic moments and solitary dinners. They articulated my obsession with particular ingredients – artichokes, fennel, the unloved pea. They traced my journeys to the source of special ingredients, recorded triumphs over unavailability and celebrated the seasons. Most of all, they seemed to chart my life.

I have cooked all these recipes again, partly because they had to be tested and perfected, but also because they are a part of my life, a part of my history. Cooking them again – some familiar, some forgotten – flooded me with recollections and affirmed my already unshakeable love of food and of cooking.

All the recipes in this book are easily achievable in a standard kitchen, which is where I cook them, and I don't have a wok burner, a char-grill or a deep-fryer. You will cook them differently, and make them your own, and that is how it should be.

Beginnings

The start of a meal excites me the most, perhaps because I enjoy having a variety of small dishes, or because I like the simplicity and self-contained quality of 'starters', or simply because that's when I'm the hungriest.

The following recipes comprise a loose selection of small meals (though some, if not many, could easily be promoted to the main event): entrees, antipasti, snacks, breakfast/brunch items and the like. They are drawn from classic combinations of ingredients and, of course, my own curiosity. Salads, light pastas, rillettes, cured salmon, carpaccio, pizza and good old chicken soup all find a place. They can be appreciated as a light meal, or as a formal entree at the start of a feast. Many of the dishes rely on the quality of produce and are therefore governed by the seasons, but with experience and experimentation you can often find alternative ingredients that produce an equally delicious result.

This section also introduces those things that are important to me and common factors in my food. Many of my recipes ask for lots of fresh herbs, lemon juice, garlic and chilli, and I favour seasonal produce, demand organic chicken and avoid ingredients added for aesthetics or fashion. I like flavourful food: complex, but clear and fresh. I believe that to cook is an act of generosity, and that the food you prepare and serve should always reflect this.

White gazpacho with prawns and avocado
This chilled soup is light, fresh and a breeze to prepare. Chop all your ingredients in advance and then simply blitz.

½ cup (80 g) blanched almonds, roughly chopped

1 clove garlic, sliced

1 green capsicum, seeded and chopped

2 green chillies, chopped, seeds left in

2 Lebanese cucumbers, peeled and coarsely chopped

1 large ripe tomato, peeled and coarsely chopped

2 slices white bread, crusts removed

1 tablespoon chopped red onion

100 ml extra virgin olive oil

salt flakes and freshly ground black pepper

½ ripe avocado

½ lemon

4 cooked king prawns, peeled, deveined, split lengthways and chopped

green Tabasco sauce, to taste

sherry vinegar, to taste

4 sprigs watercress, to serve

1 tablespoon extra virgin olive oil, extra

To make the gazpacho, put almonds, garlic and 250 ml water in a small saucepan over medium heat. Bring to the boil and cook for 6–8 minutes or until water has evaporated. Cool.

Place almond mixture, capsicum, chilli, cucumber, tomato, bread and onion in an upright blender and blend until smooth (or place ingredients in a jug and blitz with a stick blender). Stir through 3 tablespoons of the olive oil and 50 ml water. Add seasoning to taste. Place in the fridge until chilled.

Peel and dice avocado and place in a bowl. Squeeze lemon juice over avocado, then drizzle with remaining oil. Add prawns and toss gently to combine. Add Tabasco sauce.

Stir gazpacho, then add vinegar to taste. Pour into chilled bowls and add a small scoop of prawn mixture in the centre of each. To serve, garnish with watercress and drizzle with extra olive oil. SERVES 4

Gazpacho shots This gazpacho makes a lovely cool starter or cocktail shot on a hot summer's night. Hand it around to your guests in frozen shot glasses. If you like, you could also spike the gazpacho with your favourite ice-cold vodka.

Chicken and broken-pasta soup

This chicken noodle soup is guaranteed to ward off the chills and hit the spot on a lazy Sunday evening, or is perfect for a light dinner.

80 g fresh breadcrumbs

150 g chicken mince

pinch nutmeg

3 sprigs thyme

8 sprigs flat-leaf parsley, chopped

1 egg

salt flakes and freshly ground black pepper

100 ml extra virgin olive oil

2 brown onions, chopped

8 cloves garlic, chopped

2 sticks celery, chopped

¼ Savoy cabbage, shredded

200 g broken pasta (such as snapped spaghetti)
   or stelline (small, star-shaped pasta)

8 cups (2 litres) chicken stock

25 g parmesan, grated, to serve

squeeze of lemon, to serve

Place breadcrumbs, chicken mince, nutmeg, thyme, half the parsley, egg, salt and pepper in a food processor. Process until mixture forms a smooth paste. Shape mixture into small balls, about the size of a 10 cent piece, and set aside.

Heat olive oil in a large pan over low heat. Add onion, garlic, celery and a pinch of salt and cook gently for 15 minutes. Add cabbage, pasta and stock, bring to the boil and simmer for 4 minutes. Place chicken meatballs into soup and simmer for 10 minutes.

Serve soup topped with remaining parsley, parmesan and a squeeze of lemon.

SERVES 6

Stracciatella

A super-quick soup if you have chicken stock on hand, stracciatella is said to fix almost any ailment and soothe the soul. Perfect.

½ cup (110 g) risoni or stelline (star-shaped) pasta

5 cups (1.25 litres) chicken stock (preferably homemade)

4 free-range eggs

150 g freshly grated parmesan

2 teaspoons plain flour

½ bunch flat-leaf parsley leaves, chopped

salt flakes and freshly ground black pepper

extra virgin olive oil, to serve

crusty bread, to serve

Cook pasta in a saucepan of boiling water over medium heat for 5 minutes. Drain. Bring stock to the boil in a large saucepan over high heat. Place eggs, parmesan, flour and parsley in a bowl. Whisk with a fork and season with salt and pepper.

Add cooked pasta to stock. When stock returns to the boil, add egg mixture and stir with a fork. When egg mixture floats to the top, remove pan from heat, check seasoning and stir to distribute egg mixture through stock.

Serve immediately, drizzled with olive oil and accompanied by crusty bread.

SERVES 4

Stock

It's well worth the time to make your own stock by boiling a small, whole free-range chicken in water with plenty of herbs and garlic. When cooked, strain the broth and shred the chicken. Before adding the eggs to the stracciatella, return shredded chicken to the soup and add a handful of frozen peas – this is slightly more substantial and just delicious.

Spinach and lentil soup with ricotta and pancetta bruschetta

This soup has appeared on many of my menus over the years. It has a slightly earthy quality to it, and is a lovely way to start a meal.

¾ cup (150 g) Australian puy lentils, soaked in hot water for 20 minutes, drained

2 tablespoons olive oil

1 carrot, peeled and chopped

3 sticks inner celery, sliced

1 large brown onion, chopped

salt flakes

1 bay leaf

2 sprigs thyme

freshly ground black pepper

4 cups (1 litre) chicken stock

4 cloves garlic, finely chopped

1 bunch English spinach, washed and trimmed

½ bunch flat-leaf parsley leaves, coarsely chopped

2 sprigs oregano, chopped

ricotta and pancetta bruschetta

8 thin slices pancetta

4 slices ciabatta or sourdough bread

1 clove garlic

extra virgin olive oil

100 g ricotta

Place lentils in a medium-sized saucepan and cover with cold water. Bring to the boil and simmer over medium heat for 10 minutes. Drain.

In a large saucepan, heat 1 tablespoon of the olive oil over low heat. Add carrot, celery and onion and stir for 6 minutes or until vegetables are soft but not coloured. Season with a little salt, add bay leaf, thyme, drained lentils, pepper and stock, then simmer for about 25 minutes or until lentils and vegetables are tender.

Place the remaining olive oil in a frying pan and cook garlic and spinach leaves over medium heat for about 6 minutes or until the spinach has wilted. Add parsley and oregano and stir for about 6 minutes or until the parsley has wilted. Remove from heat. Add spinach mixture to stock and stir. In a food processor or blender, blend soup in batches until smooth.

Meanwhile, place pancetta under a preheated hot grill and cook for 4–5 minutes, until crisp. Toast bread under grill until golden, then rub one side very gently with a garlic clove and drizzle with your favourite olive oil. Smear generously with ricotta, top with pancetta, drop into the soup and serve immediately. SERVES 4

Bruschetta

Bruschetta is a tasty addition to any soup. To make it, simply slice ciabatta or sourdough bread thickly. Toast on both sides. Rub one side with a peeled and cut garlic clove, then drizzle generously with olive oil.

Potato soup with buttered oysters and bruschetta

This is one sexy soup. It has fared extremely well on the Melbourne Wine Room menu, and is a constant winner at dinner parties at home

50 g butter

50 ml extra virgin olive oil

6 cloves garlic, chopped

10 golden shallots, sliced

2 leeks, finely sliced

700 g desiree potatoes, peeled and
　finely sliced

6 cups (1.5 litres) fish stock

400 ml pouring cream

salt flakes and freshly ground black pepper

4 slices sourdough, toasted, brushed
　with olive oil and rubbed with garlic

1 small bunch watercress sprigs

100 g crème fraîche

extra virgin olive oil, to serve

buttered oysters

100 g unsalted butter

12 Pacific oysters, freshly shucked,
　shells removed

1 lemon, juiced

Heat butter and olive oil in a large heavy-based pan over low heat. Add garlic, shallots and leek and cook gently for 5–8 minutes, until soft but not coloured. Add potato and cook for 5 minutes. Pour in stock, bring to the boil and simmer for about 10 minutes or until vegetables are tender. Stir in cream and cook for 5 minutes. Place mixture in a food processor or blender and purée, then push through a fine strainer. Season with salt and pepper.

To make buttered oysters, heat butter and a little juice from the oysters in a small pan over low heat. Add oysters and lemon juice and cook for ½ minute or until warm.

Drop sourdough toast into soup and spoon the buttered oysters on top. Garnish with watercress sprigs and a dollop of créme fraîche, drizzle with oil and serve.

SERVES 4–6

With artichoke A beautiful alternative to the potato and leek combination in this soup is to replace 300 g of potato with finely sliced Jerusalem artichoke. This gives a rich, nutty flavour that marries perfectly with the oysters.

Celeriac and rice brodo with ricotta bruschetta

This soup is comfort food at its best. When you add the celeriac and fennel, be sure to let them caramelise in the pot to develop that rich, nutty character; the more slowly the caramelisation takes place, the more intense the flavour will be.

1¼ cups (250 g) arborio rice

½ cup (125 ml) extra virgin olive oil,
  plus extra to serve

2 large brown onions, finely sliced

5 cloves garlic, finely sliced

1 bay leaf

salt flakes and freshly ground black pepper

2 celeriacs, peeled and cut into 1 cm pieces

1 bulb fennel, trimmed and finely chopped,
  fronds reserved

6 cups (1.5 litres) chicken stock

4 cups (1 litre) water

½ bunch flat-leaf parsley leaves,
  finely chopped

2½ teaspoons ground fennel seeds

ricotta bruschetta

200 g ricotta

8 slices crusty bread, toasted, brushed
  with olive oil and rubbed with garlic

Cook rice in a large saucepan of lightly salted boiling water over medium heat for 5 minutes. Drain.

Heat olive oil in a large heavy-based saucepan over low heat. Add onion, garlic, bay leaf, salt and pepper and cook for 10 minutes, stirring occasionally. Add celeriac and fennel and cook for 25 minutes, stirring occasionally, until golden. Add rice, stock, water, parsley, fennel seeds and fronds from the fennel (reserve a few for serving). Stir and simmer for 12–15 minutes or until rice is cooked and soup has thickened.

Remove from heat and set aside for 10 minutes to allow to cool a little. Purée in a food processor or with a stick blender; if the soup is too thick, add a little extra water. Spread ricotta on toasted bread and sprinkle with extra fennel tops and black pepper. To serve, drizzle extra olive oil over the soup, sprinkle with salt flakes and serve bruschetta alongside. SERVES 8

Celeriac Celeriac is the perfect companion to grilled beef. Simply grate it using the finest side of the grater and grate some fresh horseradish to go with it. Using a three-to-one ratio, mix extra virgin olive oil with lemon and mustard. Toss the dressing through the celeriac and horseradish, and use as a condiment, such as mustard.

Pasta e fagioli This is a meal in itself if you serve it with bruschetta in the bottom of the bowl. It is best served the day after making; store cooled soup in the fridge and reheat over low heat.

1 cup (200 g) dried cannellini beans,
   soaked in cold water overnight, drained

50 ml olive oil

2 cloves garlic, finely chopped

3 brown onions, finely chopped

1 small red chilli, finely chopped

1 sprig thyme

1 bay leaf

2 stems cavolo nero (see glossary) or 1 leaf
   silver beet, chopped

2 small carrots, peeled and finely chopped

2 sticks celery, finely chopped

100 g pancetta, cut into 3 cm pieces

½ bulb fennel, finely chopped,
   fronds reserved

1 tablespoon tomato paste

⅓ cup (75 g) macaroni or tubetti pasta

8 cups (2 litres) chicken stock

½ bunch flat-leaf parsley leaves

2 tablespoons fresh or frozen peas

6 slices sourdough bread, toasted, rubbed
   lightly with garlic and drizzled with olive oil

extra virgin olive oil, to serve

Place soaked cannellini beans in a large saucepan, cover with cold water and bring to the boil. Cook for about 40 minutes or until tender. Drain and reserve 1 cup of cooking liquid.

Pour olive oil into a large saucepan and place over low heat. Add garlic, onion, chilli, thyme and bay leaf and stir for 8 minutes or until onion is soft. Add cavolo nero, carrot, celery, pancetta and half the fennel and stir to combine. Cook for about 20 minutes, stirring occasionally, until the vegetables have caramelised. Add remaining fennel, tomato paste, pasta, stock, parsley, cannellini beans and reserved cooking liquid. Bring soup to the boil and simmer for 5 minutes. Remove from heat. Add a little extra water at this stage if you think the soup is too thick.

To serve, reheat soup over low heat. A few minutes before you are ready to eat, add peas and fennel fronds. Place bruschetta in the bottom of warmed bowls and pour soup over the top. Drizzle with a little extra virgin olive oil and serve with extra bruschetta on the side. SERVES 6

Lamb shanks with pearl barley and lentils

70 ml extra virgin olive oil

2 lamb shanks, cut into 3 cm pieces
   (ask your butcher to do this)

salt flakes

1½ brown onions, halved and finely sliced

3 cloves garlic, finely chopped

2 small red chillies (or to taste), split

1 teaspoon ground cumin

½ teaspoon ground cinnamon

½ teaspoon freshly ground black pepper

½ teaspoon ground coriander

½ teaspoon caraway seeds

pinch saffron threads

150 g celeriac, peeled and chopped

2 carrots, peeled and sliced

3 sticks celery, sliced

1 × 400 g can tomatoes

8 cups (2 litres) water

1 beef stock cube

½ cup (100 g) pearl barley

50 g lentils

50 g canned chickpeas, drained

30 g fresh or frozen peas

½ bunch mint leaves

½ bunch coriander leaves

½ bunch flat-leaf parsley leaves

⅓ cup (95 g) sheep's milk yoghurt

½ lemon, juiced

Lamb shanks with pearl barley and lentils This is my ultimate winter soup. The dish is inspired by the North African harira, a soup eaten after night-fall during Ramadan. It can be made of meat or vegetables and is cooked for hours in a clay pot that sits on the embers of a fire. In my version I have used all the traditional spices, vegetables and grains, and have added lamb shanks and pearl barley, which enrich the soup. Make a big pot and your loved ones will think you are the best, as this soup is yummy, nourishing and addictive. An added bonus is that it freezes beautifully.

Heat olive oil in a large, heavy-based ovenproof dish over medium heat. Add lamb, sprinkle lightly with salt and brown on all sides. Add onion, garlic, chillies and spices and stir well. Add fresh vegetables and cook, stirring occasionally, for 5–6 minutes. Add tomatoes and their juice, water, crumbled stock cube, barley, lentils and chickpeas. Bring to a simmer over medium heat.

Cover the dish, reduce heat to very low and simmer for about 2½–3 hours or until meat is very tender and falling off the bone. (If you prefer, you can bake in the oven at 140°C for 2–2½ hours.)

Stir in peas and check seasoning. To serve, sprinkle with herbs, and top with a dollop of yoghurt and a squeeze of lemon juice. SERVES 4

Basic pizza dough

This never-fail pizza dough is a home variation on the dough we serve at mr wolf, my pizzeria in Melbourne.

400 g plain flour (preferably unbleached)

100 g fine semolina

2 teaspoons table salt

1½ cups (375 ml) warm water

3 tablespoons olive oil

2 teaspoons (7 g) dried yeast

Combine flour, semolina and salt in the bowl of an electric mixer with dough hook attached (see below). Mix water, oil and yeast in a small bowl and stir to dissolve yeast. Pour water mixture into flour and mix at low speed until combined, then mix on high speed for 10 minutes until dough is smooth and elastic, but still quite wet and sticky.

Place dough in a lightly oiled bowl. Cover with plastic film and rest in a warm place for about 30 minutes or until dough has doubled in size.

Divide into four portions. The dough can be used at once or stored, covered, in the fridge overnight. MAKES 4 PIZZA BASES

Pizza dough If preparing dough for the next day, use cold water in the dough and prove it in the fridge overnight.

If you don't have a dough hook, combine basic dough ingredients and gather mixture into a ball. On a smooth surface lightly dusted with flour, knead for 15 minutes or until dough is smooth, elastic and sticky.

> Pizza no. 9 at mr wolf

This combination is all about simple, fresh ingredients that are a perfect marriage made in pizza heaven.

olive oil and fine semolina, to coat pizza tray

1 portion basic pizza dough

⅓ cup (80 ml) extra virgin olive oil

150 g buffalo mozzarella, sliced

100 g mozzarella, sliced

freshly ground black pepper

½ lemon, juiced

80 g rocket leaves

6 slices prosciutto

Preheat oven to 250°C. Lightly brush a large pizza tray with oil and dust with semolina. Roll pizza dough out on a lightly floured surface and transfer to the pizza tray.

Drizzle pizza base with half the oil and top with cheeses. Season with pepper and bake for 10–15 minutes until dough is golden and cheese has almost totally melted.

Whisk lemon juice with remaining oil. Dress rocket leaves in a small bowl and toss to combine. Remove pizza from oven and cut it, then immediately lay slices of prosciutto and dressed rocket on top and serve. MAKES 1 LARGE PIZZA. SERVES 4–6

Timing This dough and topping work wonderfully in those new-fangled home pizza chef ovens, but note that cooking times will be shorter, and you will yield more pizzas, as these pizza oven bases are quite small.

Potato focaccia with tomato, oregano and black olives

The focaccia will keep for a few days in the fridge – just reheat for 10 minutes in a hot oven to freshen it up. Or, if you are like me, just eat it straight from the oven. I like to cut a slice and throw it back in the oven to crisp up the bottom.

2 medium desiree potatoes, peeled, boiled until tender, drained and used hot

500 g plain flour

2 teaspoons salt flakes

1½ cups (375 ml) warm water

1½ teaspoons (5 g) dried yeast

2 tablespoons extra virgin olive oil

½ bunch basil leaves, torn

1 bunch oregano leaves, coarsely chopped

½ cup (80 g) pitted black olives, chopped

3 ripe tomatoes, diced

freshly ground black pepper

Use a vegetable mouli or potato ricer to purée the hot potato, then place it in the bowl of an electric mixer with dough hook attached. Add flour and salt and mix to combine. Place water and yeast in a small bowl and stir to dissolve yeast. Add all water mixture at once to potato mixture and mix on low speed until combined, then mix on high speed for 10 minutes until dough is smooth and elastic. Don't panic if the dough is wet and sticky – that's what gives this focaccia its awesome airy and crispy texture.

Transfer dough to a lightly oiled bowl, cover with plastic film and rest in a warm place for 40 minutes until doubled in size. Lightly brush a non-stick baking tray (about 30 × 40 cm) with oil. Press dough onto the tray, then drizzle with 1 tablespoon oil. Cover lightly with plastic film and leave to rise in a warm place for 20–25 minutes or until doubled in size.

Preheat oven to 180°C.

For the topping, combine basil, oregano, olives and tomato in a medium bowl. Pour in remaining olive oil, season with pepper and toss to coat. Scatter tomato mixture over focaccia and bake for 30–40 minutes or until golden and cooked. Set aside to rest for 15 minutes. Remove from tray, place on racks in the oven for a few minutes to re-crisp, and serve. MAKES 1 LARGE FOCACCIA. SERVES 6.

Smoked trout, kipfler and avocado salad with horseradish mayo

This sublime salad can be assembled on individual plates for a dinner party, or piled on a platter for a more casual BBQ. It is really worth sourcing fresh horseradish for this dish. I just love its peppery, pungent flavour – it's almost addictive.

5 large kipfler potatoes, peeled

⅓ cup (80 ml) extra virgin olive oil

salt flakes and freshly ground black pepper

1 bulb fennel

2 tablespoons cornflour

1 cup (250 ml) canola oil

½ bunch watercress or curly endive

1 witlof, thinly sliced

½ bunch chives, chopped

1 lemon, juiced

1 large ripe avocado, thinly sliced

1 smoked trout or 4 fillets, flaked

horseradish mayo

½ cup (150 g) good-quality mayonnaise

½ cup (140 g) Greek-style yoghurt

100 g finely grated horseradish root
  or 4 tablespoons horseradish sauce
  (or to taste)

Place potatoes in a medium-sized saucepan of lightly salted water and bring to the boil. Cook for 10–15 minutes or until tender. Drain potatoes and slice on the diagonal. Toss with 2 tablespoons of the olive oil, season with salt and pepper and keep warm.

Trim top, bottom and any damaged portions of the fennel, cut in half and slice thinly. Reserve the fronds. Dust half the fennel slices in cornflour. Heat the canola oil in a frying pan over medium heat. Fry the dusted fennel slices until golden. Place on kitchen paper to drain. Season with salt and pepper. Combine remaining fennel slices and reserved fronds in a bowl with watercress, witlof and chives. Drizzle with remaining olive oil and half the lemon juice. Toss gently to combine.

To make the horseradish mayo, place mayonnaise, yoghurt and horseradish in a small bowl and stir well.

To serve, divide potato slices among 4 plates and spread with horseradish mayo. Top with avocado and flaked trout. Arrange fried fennel around salad and place watercress mixture on top of trout. Drizzle remaining lemon juice over salad and serve. SERVES 4

Horseradish mayo Keep leftover horseradish mayonnaise in the fridge for a couple of days and spread on roast chicken sandwiches.

Caesar salad

Classic Caesar salad is one of the great favourites. The better the mayonnaise, the better the salad – make your own if possible. If the other ingredients are also top quality, you're more than halfway there.

1 bulb garlic

1 cup (300 g) egg mayonnaise

2 tablespoons sour cream

8 anchovy fillets, finely chopped

½ lemon, juiced

½ clove garlic, finely chopped

splash of vinegar

4 free-range eggs (60 g each)

3 baby cos lettuces, very outer leaves removed and each cut into 6 wedges, leaving core intact

½ cup flat-leaf parsley leaves, finely chopped

½ bunch chives, finely chopped

1 red onion, finely sliced

3 tablespoons small capers

10 slices pancetta, roasted at 165°C for 5–7 minutes

150 g shaved parmesan

extra lemon juice

freshly ground black pepper

4 slices sourdough bread

extra clove garlic and olive oil, to serve

To make the dressing, roast the garlic bulb at 150°C for 30 minutes, then cut and squeeze flesh out. Combine roasted garlic flesh, mayonnaise, sour cream, anchovies, lemon juice and chopped garlic in a food processor and process until smooth. If the mix is too stiff, add a little lemon juice until dressing is sauce-like. Set aside.

Bring a saucepan of lightly salted water to the boil and add a splash of vinegar. Slide in eggs and poach for 3–5 minutes. Remove with a slotted spoon and keep warm.

Arrange lettuce on plates and drizzle over dressing. Scatter parsley, chives, onion and capers over lettuce.

Place an egg on each plate, crumble pancetta over eggs, shave over some parmesan, add a squeeze of extra lemon juice and, if desired, grind over black pepper.

Toast the bread, rub with an extra clove of garlic, then drizzle with olive oil and cut into fingers. Serve immediately. SERVES 4

Perfect poached eggs

To poach the perfect egg, you need the freshest and best free-range eggs you can get your hands on, a deep but small pot of hot water just off the boil with a splash of vinegar and salt added, and a slotted spoon to stir the water in a whirlpool motion (and to carefully lift out the egg). Simply slip your egg into the spinning water and poach for 3–5 minutes.

Panzanella

This traditional Italian peasant salad, made with stale bread and very ripe tomatoes, is very robust. I like to eat it on its own on a summer's afternoon when tomatoes and basil are at their best and just too good to resist.

4 very ripe vine-ripened tomatoes,
    coarsely chopped

1 clove garlic, finely chopped

30 basil leaves, torn

⅓ cup (80 ml) red-wine vinegar

150 ml extra virgin olive oil

1 celery heart, sliced, and leaves

150 g coarsely grated parmigiano reggiano

½ red onion, sliced

5–6 slices day-old thick, crusty sourdough bread,
    torn into small chunks

salt flakes and freshly ground black pepper

extra virgin olive oil, red-wine vinegar and
    parmigiano reggiano, to serve

Place tomatoes, garlic, basil, vinegar, oil, celery, parmigiano, onion and bread in a large bowl. Toss gently to combine, then add extra olive oil and vinegar and generous amounts of salt and black pepper. Shave over extra parmigiano reggiano.
SERVES 4

Seasoning The salad should be sharp and well seasoned – leave it to sit for 10 minutes for flavours to develop, then adjust final seasoning before eating. Panzanella goes well with pan-seared fish.

Corella pear, pecorino, walnut and currant salad

Take the classic combination of pear and cheese to another level by adding toasted walnuts and a delicious mix of pickled onions, currants simmered in vinegar and peppery cress.

6 corella pears, cored and cut into 5 mm slices

½ lemon, juiced

⅓ cup (80 ml) extra virgin olive oil

50 g currants, simmered in 1 tablespoon
    red-wine vinegar for 1 minute, then drained

salt flakes and freshly ground black pepper

1 bunch watercress

3 tablespoons small pickled onions, halved

1 cup (100 g) toasted walnuts, coarsely chopped

2 tablespoons sour cream

2 tablespoons water

1 tablespoon red-wine vinegar

1 punnet mustard cress

100 g pecorino cheese (see glossary), shaved

Place pear slices, lemon juice and 1 tablespoon olive oil in a medium-sized bowl. Toss gently to combine. Stir through the currants and season with salt and pepper. Trim the watercress and break into small sprigs. Arrange sprigs over a platter and top with pears. Scatter onions and walnuts over the top.

To make the dressing, combine sour cream, remaining olive oil, water and vinegar in a bowl and mix until smooth. Pour dressing over salad, toss gently and scatter with mustard cress and shavings of pecorino. SERVES 4–6

Genovese salad This salad was named after Genoa in Italy, where pesto originated. Take it to the next BBQ you go to and let the old standard potato salad take a back seat. It adds a whole new dimension to lamb chops, veal, steak or whole baked fish, or you can just have it on its own.

pesto

1 large bunch basil (100 g),
    coarsely chopped

¼ bunch flat-leaf parsley (20 g),
    coarsely chopped

1 small clove garlic, sliced

100 g grated parmesan

40 g pine nuts

100 ml extra virgin olive oil

salt flakes and freshly ground black pepper

salad

6 small desiree potatoes

50 ml extra virgin olive oil

50 ml red-wine vinegar

200 g green beans, trimmed

½ cup fresh or frozen peas

200 g lasagnette or dried pappardelle,
    broken into pieces

100 ml pesto

1 cup spinach leaves, shredded

30 g pine nuts

salt flakes and freshly ground
    black pepper

To make the pesto, place all ingredients in the bowl of a food processor and blend to a thick, smooth paste. (Makes about 1 cup.)

To make the salad, cook potatoes in a medium-sized saucepan of lightly salted boiling water for 10–15 minutes or until tender. Drain, reserving cooking liquid. Slice potatoes thickly and toss with 2 tablespoons of the olive oil and the vinegar.

Cook beans in lightly salted boiling water for about 3 minutes, or until just cooked. Drain. Cook peas in reserved cooking liquid for 1 minute. Drain. Cook pasta in lightly salted boiling water until just past al dente. Drain, then transfer to a bowl and stir through the remaining oil and half the pesto. Add shredded spinach to hot pasta and stir through until wilted. Add potatoes, beans and peas and remaining pesto and pine nuts and stir to combine. Season with salt and pepper. Serve at room temperature. SERVES 4–6

Pesto Pesto is amazingly versatile – it can be spread on fresh crusty bread, tossed through pasta or used as a marinade for fish or meat. You can even stir it through cooked scrambled eggs. The parsley in the recipe turns it a gorgeous, vivid bright green.

If you're keeping pesto in a jar, smooth the top and pour a little olive oil over it to form a seal.

Curly endive, bacon and egg salad I love this dish. Often people don't like curly endive because they find it bitter, which can be the case if the leaves are not dressed properly. In this salad, the bitter endive complements the bacon and egg perfectly, with the golden shallots and Jerusalem artichokes adding flavour and texture. The bacon fat makes an instant dressing – don't be scared to use it.

8 golden shallots, peeled

4 cloves garlic

3 tablespoons extra virgin olive oil

300 g curly endive leaves (use only the light green and delicate yellow leaves), washed and torn

3 Jerusalem artichokes, peeled, finely sliced and mixed with a squeeze of lemon juice

3 eggs, soft-boiled (use hot water from the tap, then cook on high heat for 6 minutes)

200 g thick rindless bacon, cut into 3 cm pieces

3 cloves garlic, finely sliced

salt flakes and freshly ground black pepper

½ lemon

4 slices sourdough bread, toasted, rubbed lightly with 1 clove garlic, drizzled with 2 tablespoons olive oil, and cut into fingers

Preheat oven to 180°C. Toss golden shallots and garlic in olive oil. Place in a baking dish and roast for 25 minutes. Arrange curly endive on a platter. Scatter golden shallots and artichokes over endive. Cut tops from eggs and spoon eggs onto salad.

Heat a non-stick frying pan, then cook bacon over medium heat for 6–8 minutes or until crisp. Add garlic and stir for 1 minute. Pour bacon, garlic and bacon fat over salad. Season and squeeze over lemon juice. Serve with toast on the side. SERVES 4–6

Dressing salads Dressing well is the secret to enjoying bitter leaves such as endive, witlof and radicchio – they must be well coated and seasoned. Try using your favourite balsamic vinegar if you'd prefer more sweetness. Seeded mustard is another good addition to the dressing. Always wash your leaves thoroughly, and make sure they are dry before dressing with hot ingredients.

Insalata caprese This classic salad is enhanced by the quality of the tomatoes and oil you use. Mozzarella, or fiore di latte ('flower of milk'), is a soft cow's or buffalo milk cheese, about the size of a tennis ball. It should be sweet smelling.

3 long, fat red chillies

3 large (120 g each) fresh mozzarella (*fiore di latte*), sliced

3 tablespoons natural yoghurt

50 ml extra virgin olive oil

salt flakes and freshly ground black pepper

4 medium vine-ripened
    ox-heart tomatoes, sliced

½ red onion, finely chopped

20 basil leaves, bruised in a mortar and pestle
    with ½ garlic clove and 100 ml olive oil

3 tablespoons aged balsamic vinegar

crusty bread, to serve

extra basil leaves (optional), to serve

Preheat oven to 150°C. Place chillies on a lightly greased baking tray and bake for about 15 minutes or until skins are loose. (You can also cook the chillies on a lightly greased barbecue plate preheated to medium.) When chillies are cool enough to handle, remove skins and slice into strips.

Slice or tear cheeses into strips. Place in a medium-sized bowl with yoghurt, olive oil, salt and pepper and stir to combine. Arrange tomatoes on a platter and top with cheese mix. Sprinkle the finely chopped onion and the chilli strips on top. Drizzle with smashed basil and oil mixture and balsamic vinegar. Scatter extra basil leaves over the salad, if desired and serve with crusty bread. SERVES 4–6

Buffalo mozzarella Buffalo mozzarella in Italy is the softest, milkiest pillow of cheese you'll ever taste. Australian buffalo mozzarella is good but does have a different consistency to the Italian cheese, which is why I decided to bathe the fiore di latte in yoghurt and extra virgin olive oil, to enrich it for the caprese.

Barley-almond tabbouleh with sumac-spiced prawns

This is one of my twists on tabbouleh, using barley. It's unusual to serve tabbouleh with prawns but it works a treat. Sumac and cinnamon are the magic ingredients, and the boiled barley has a sexy, slippery texture. Serve it on a big platter and let everyone help themselves.

1 cup (200 g) pearl barley

1 cinnamon stick

1 lemon, juiced

100 ml extra virgin olive oil

2 teaspoons ground cumin mixed with
   1 tablespoon salt flakes

freshly ground black pepper

1 cup coriander leaves, torn

2 cups flat-leaf parsley leaves, torn

3 cups watercress, coarsely chopped

1 red onion, finely sliced

1 celery heart, finely chopped,
   yellow leaves reserved

¾ cup (120 g) almonds, toasted (skin on)
   and coarsely chopped

¾ cup (200 g) plain yoghurt

spiced prawns

8 large green (raw) prawns, peeled,
   with tails intact

squeeze of lemon

1 tablespoon sumac (see glossary)

1 teaspoon ground cumin

1 lemon, zested

4 red chillies, finely chopped

Place barley and cinnamon stick in a medium-sized saucepan. Cover with water and bring to the boil over medium heat. Simmer for 20–30 minutes or until barley is cooked and tender. Drain the barley, then stir through lemon juice, half the olive oil and combined cumin and salt. Season with pepper. Keep warm.

To make spiced prawns, bring a saucepan of lightly salted water to the boil over medium heat. Drop in the prawns and add a squeeze of lemon. Simmer for 2 minutes or until prawns just change colour. Drain, then toss with remaining olive oil, sumac, cumin, lemon zest and chilli. Set aside for 10 minutes.

To make tabbouleh, combine the barley mixture with herbs, watercress, onion, celery heart and leaves and 80 g of the almonds. Season to taste.

Spread yoghurt on a serving platter and top with tabbouleh. Arrange prawns on top and scatter over remaining almonds. SERVES 4

Spicy sausage with lentil and cavolo nero salad

This is a terrific winter weekend salad, just right for lunch or a light dinner. Serve it with crusty bread and your favourite mustard on the side. I also like to add a dollop of fresh goat's cheese.

2½ cups (500 g) Australian puy lentils

½ cup (125 ml) extra virgin olive oil

10 golden shallots, finely sliced

2 cloves garlic, finely sliced

1 bay leaf

2 cups (500 ml) hot chicken stock

salt flakes and freshly ground black pepper

6–8 thin merguez or spicy chorizo sausages

50 ml sherry vinegar

250 g cavolo nero leaves (see glossary)
    or baby spinach leaves

1 cup flat-leaf parsley leaves

1 punnet baby red basil leaves or
    ½ bunch red or green basil leaves (see glossary)

100 g canned baby artichoke hearts, drained

crusty bread, to serve

mustard, to serve

goat's cheese (optional), to serve

Blanch lentils in a saucepan of boiling water for 1–2 minutes, then drain and set aside. Heat 2 tablespoons olive oil in a medium pan over medium heat. Add golden shallots, garlic and bay leaf and cook for 2 minutes. Add lentils, pour in stock and simmer for 12–15 minutes or until lentils are tender and stock is absorbed. Season with salt and pepper. Allow to cool slightly.

Preheat grill to high. Prick sausages with a knife, then grill for 10 minutes or until cooked through. Slice in half lengthways.

To make the dressing, whisk remaining olive oil and the vinegar until combined. Place cavolo nero or spinach, parsley, red basil, lentils and dressing in a large bowl and stir until combined. Place half the salad on a platter and lay sausages on top. Scatter over remaining salad and place artichokes on top.

Serve with bread, mustard, and goat's cheese, if desired. SERVES 4–6

Sicilian spaghetti al'olio

Toasted, seasoned breadcrumbs, which the Italians call pangrattato, give an unexpected crunch to pasta. In the south of Italy, crumbs are also known as 'poor man's parmesan'. The addition of lemon gives the chilli and garlic a gentle zing.

500 g fresh spaghetti

½ cup (125 ml) extra virgin olive oil

2 cloves garlic, very finely sliced

2 small red chillies, very finely sliced

2 handfuls spinach, chopped

1 handful flat-leaf parsley leaves, torn

1 lemon, juiced and zested

salt flakes and freshly ground black pepper

10 thin slices sourdough baguette,
    fried in oil until crisp and seasoned, then
    pulsed in a food processor until crumbed

parmigiano reggiano, finely grated

Cook spaghetti in a large saucepan of lightly salted boiling water for 5–8 minutes or until al dente. Drain.

Heat half the oil in a large non-stick frying pan over medium heat. Add garlic and chilli and cook for 1–2 minutes. Add spinach, parsley and lemon zest and stir. Season with salt and pepper. Remove from heat. Add pasta to frying pan with lemon juice and remaining oil. Add sourdough crumbs and toss to combine. Check seasoning. Serve immediately with the parmigiano reggiano. SERVES 4

> Angel-hair pasta with butter, soft goat's curd, chervil and chives

I find that goat's curd and fresh herbs are at their peak during spring and summer. Lash out and buy the best goat's curd you can find – it's wickedly addictive.

150 g cultured unsalted butter

500 g fresh angel-hair pasta

½ cup chives, finely chopped

¾ cup chervil, coarsely chopped

150 g fresh soft goat's curd or
    marinated soft goat's fetta, crumbled

salt flakes and freshly ground black pepper

extra virgin olive oil, for drizzling

shaved parmesan (optional), to serve

Cut butter into small cubes and set aside at room temperature for about 20 minutes.

Cook pasta in a large saucepan of lightly salted boiling water for 2–3 minutes or until al dente. Drain, then add butter and toss to combine. Stir through chives, chervil and goat's cheese. Season with salt and cracked pepper. Drizzle generously with extra virgin olive oil. Serve immediately, scattered with parmesan, if desired. SERVES 4

Carpaccio of yellowfin with radicchio, cream, fried capers and egg

This classic carpaccio makes an appearance every summer at the Melbourne Wine Room. I usually buy yellowfin tuna because it is well priced, has that beautiful jewel colour and tastes great. Buy it fresh and use it on the same day. Quality extra virgin olive oil and generous amounts of lemon juice are essential in this recipe, and the little touch of cream enriches the whole dish, so be sure to use it.

400 g yellowfin tuna

salt flakes and freshly ground black pepper

½ red onion, finely chopped

8 small radicchio leaves, torn

2 eggs, hard-boiled

2 tablespoons capers, fried

3 tablespoons pouring cream

½ cup (125 ml) extra virgin olive oil

1 lemon, cut into wedges

crusty bread or grissini, to serve

lemon wedges, to serve

Cut tuna into 4 slices. Place each slice between 2 sheets of baking paper and, using a rolling pin, press to flatten until it is double the size. Place tuna on 4 chilled plates and season with salt and pepper.

Sprinkle onion over tuna, then radicchio. Grate eggs over tuna and scatter fried capers over the top. Drizzle with cream and oil and squeeze lemon over tuna. Serve with crusty bread or grissini and lemon wedges. SERVES 4

Ocean trout rillettes

Ocean trout rillettes beats any store-bought fish paste or pâté. Spread it on fresh or toasted bread or on crackers, or shape spoonfuls into quenelles (use two dessertspoons to make football shapes) and serve cradled in baby cos leaves with avocado, asparagus, chives and lemon.

100 g unsalted butter, softened

80 g plain yoghurt

2 egg yolks

50 ml extra virgin olive oil

2 × 250 g ocean trout fillets, pin-boned and skin removed

1 lemon, juiced

salt flakes and freshly ground black pepper

½ bunch chives, finely chopped

Place softened butter in a stainless-steel bowl and whisk until light and creamy. Add yoghurt and egg yolks and whisk again until mixture is glossy; this may take 1–2 minutes. Whisk in olive oil. Set aside at room temperature.

Halve ocean trout fillets. Pour some water with a little of the lemon juice into a deep frying pan, add a little salt, then bring to a simmer. Add ocean trout and simmer for 4–6 minutes. Remove and drain well. Set aside to rest for 5 minutes. Break the ocean trout into flakes, then stir through butter mixture. Season with salt, pepper and remaining lemon juice. Set aside for 20 minutes. Gently fold the chives through the mix and serve, ideally at room temperature. SERVES 4–6

Black mussels with chorizo, chilli, tomato and pearl pasta

This dish has been a constant winner on my menus at Icebergs and the Melbourne Wine Room. Make sure the chorizo has some age to it and is spicy (ask the experts at a good deli for advice). Use a tiny pasta so that it wriggles its way, along with the sauce, into every mussel.

100 ml olive oil

250 g hot chorizo sausage,
   finely chopped

6 golden shallots, finely sliced

3 cloves garlic, finely sliced

3 small red chillies, finely sliced

1 bay leaf

2 pinches saffron threads

2 cups tomato sugo or crushed tomato

300 g dried small pasta (such as risoni)
   or Iranian couscous (see glossary)

300 ml dry white wine

1.5 kg black mussels, scrubbed and
   beards removed

½ bunch flat-leaf parsley,
   coarsely chopped

Heat 1 tablespoon of olive oil in a large heavy-based saucepan over high heat. Fry chorizo for 6–8 minutes or until it begins to brown. Add golden shallots, garlic, chillies, bay leaf and saffron and cook, stirring occasionally, for 5 minutes. Pour in tomato sugo, stir, then simmer for 10 minutes. Remove from heat.

Add the pasta to a saucepan of lightly salted boiling water. Stir and bring the water back to the boil, then cook for 5 minutes. Drain, then mix 2 tablespoons of the olive oil through the pasta. Cover and keep warm.

Pour wine into a large saucepan and add half the mussels. Cook, covered, over high heat for 2–3 minutes or until mussels open. Remove mussels and discard any that have not opened. Repeat with remaining mussels. Remove top shell from half the mussels and reserve the cooking liquid.

Add chorizo mixture, parsley, pasta and mussels to the cooking liquid and bring to a simmer over high heat. Drizzle over remaining olive oil and serve. SERVES 4

Home-cured ocean trout Curing your own ocean trout or salmon is simple and the sweet, citrusy flavour is far superior to commercially smoked products. I like to garnish my cured salmon traditionally with crème fraîche, a poached egg, thinly sliced cucumber, capers and lemon wedges. A little caviar is decadent but completes the combination if you feel like lashing out.

1 tablespoon coriander seeds

3 teaspoons white peppercorns

150 g salt flakes

¼ cup (55 g) castor sugar

2 large lemons, juiced and zested

2 large oranges, juiced and zested

1.2 kg side of ocean trout, pin-boned, with skin on (see note)

2 teaspoons Dijon mustard

½ bunch dill, finely chopped

Place coriander seeds and peppercorns in a mortar and pestle and pound well. Transfer to a bowl and add salt, sugar, lemon and orange juice and zest and stir. Pour into a narrow plastic, glass or earthenware dish. Place ocean trout, skin-side up, in marinade. Cover dish with plastic film and refrigerate for 24 hours, turning salmon every 6–8 hours.

Remove ocean trout from marinade, wipe off excess with kitchen paper and place on a chopping board, skin-side down. Brush mustard evenly over salmon and press over dill. Wrap tightly in plastic film and refrigerate for 1 hour. To serve, cut into thin slivers on the diagonal. SERVES 8

Pin-boning fish To pin-bone fish, feel for the bones with your fingertips then use eyebrow tweezers to remove the bones one by one. Or easier still, ask your fishmonger to do it.

Barbecued blue swimmer crab This is a firm BBQ favourite at my house when we are in the mood for a crab fest. Don't be scared of getting your hands sticky. To really enjoy this dish, you have to pick up the crab pieces with your hands and munch and suck away! It's a good idea to supply finger bowls, plenty of napkins and lots of icy beer.

8 raw blue swimmer crabs

½ bunch mint leaves, torn

½ bunch coriander leaves, chopped

1 small knob fresh ginger, grated

2 small red chillies, finely sliced

1 large clove garlic, finely chopped

2 limes, juiced and zested

100 ml extra virgin olive oil

2 tablespoons fish sauce

3 tablespoons palm sugar, shaved

lime wedges, to serve

Clean crabs, cut into quarters and crack claws. Place crabs in a large bowl and add half the mint and coriander leaves. To make the marinade, place ginger, chilli, garlic, lime juice and zest, olive oil, fish sauce and palm sugar in a small bowl and stir to combine. Pour three-quarters of the marinade over crabs and toss gently to coat. Leave for 5 minutes.

Preheat barbecue until hot, then cook crabs, turning regularly, for 5–8 minutes or until just cooked through. Pour remaining marinade over crabs and sprinkle with remaining mint and coriander leaves. Serve with lime wedges. SERVES 8

Marinade This Thai-style marinade works a treat with green prawns or fish either as a marinade or sauce. Simply wrap a marinated whole fish in non-stick baking paper and foil and cook on a preheated hot barbecue flat plate for about 20 minutes (flip halfway through).

For a more substantial meal, try serving the marinated barbecued crab in the recipe above with steamed vermicelli noodles. Make an extra, separate, half-quantity of the marinade to dress the noodles. Serve the seafood on top.

Tuna niçoise

This is yet another dish close to my heart. My interpretation has evolved over the years into this perfectly layered niçoise that I'm sure will become a firm favourite of yours too. If you do not have fresh tuna, use a quality canned tuna in oil.

4 free-range eggs (60 g each)

splash of vinegar

½ bunch basil leaves, finely chopped

½ bunch flat-leaf parsley leaves, finely chopped

150 ml extra virgin olive oil

salt flakes and freshly ground black pepper

250 g small green beans, trimmed

½ red onion, thinly sliced

1 punnet (250 g) red cherry tomatoes, quartered

100 g butter, chopped

6 anchovy fillets, chopped

1 clove garlic, finely chopped

½ cup (150 g) mayonnaise

2 tablespoons plain yoghurt

4 yellowfin tuna steaks (120 g each)

3 large desiree or kipfler potatoes, peeled and boiled in lightly salted water, then thinly sliced and tossed in olive oil, salt and pepper and kept warm

1 tablespoon small capers

16 black olives

lemon wedges, to serve

Bring a saucepan of lightly salted water to the boil and add a splash of vinegar. Slide in the eggs and poach for 3–5 minutes. Remove with a slotted spoon and keep warm.

Place herbs in a bowl, add 50 ml olive oil and season with salt and pepper. Cook beans in lightly salted boiling water for 3–4 minutes. Drain and add hot beans immediately to herb and oil mix. Add onion and cherry tomatoes and toss to combine.

To make the anchovy sauce, place butter, remaining olive oil, anchovies and garlic in a small saucepan. Use a wooden spoon to stir over low heat until anchovies dissolve, then season with salt and pepper and set aside.

Mix mayonnaise and yoghurt in a separate bowl.

On a hot barbecue or in a hot non-stick pan, sear the lightly oiled tuna or cook to your liking (2–3 minutes for rare, 3–4 minutes for medium, 4–6 minutes for well done).

To serve, spread mayonnaise on four plates, arrange potato slices over and top with tuna. Spoon on the bean mix and scatter with capers and olives. Place egg on top and spoon over hot anchovy sauce. Serve immediately with lemon wedges. SERVES 4

Anchovy sauce The anchovy sauce in this recipe is fantastic with raw baby vegetables; or add chopped capers and parsley and spoon it over grilled, poached or pan-fried fish.

Scallop ceviche with sherry vinegar and green chilli

Ceviche is raw fish or seafood that is 'cooked' in a citrus marinade. Scallops cured in this manner are unusual but addictive, with a rich, citrus–caramel flavour and silky smooth texture. Use the freshest, sweetest scallops in the shell that you can find (do not attempt this recipe otherwise – the seafood needs to be absolutely fresh). Placing the scallops back in the shell to serve as an individual entrée is a great touch; rest the shell on damp salt to keep it steady on the plate. Serve lots of bread to mop up the juices.

100 ml sherry vinegar

1 lemon, juiced and zested

2 green chillies, finely sliced

2 celery hearts, finely sliced

2 Lebanese cucumbers, peeled and chopped

pinch castor sugar

150 ml extra virgin olive oil

450 g scallops

salt flakes and freshly ground black pepper

plain flour (optional), for dusting

1 baguette, thinly sliced or toasted

To make the marinade, place vinegar, lemon juice and zest, chillies, celery, cucumbers, sugar and 110 ml of olive oil in a medium bowl and stir well. Set aside for 5 minutes.

Trim scallops, removing roe if present. Place roe on kitchen paper and set aside. Slice each scallop crossways into three thin discs and arrange on a serving plate. Pour marinade over and season. Cover and place in the fridge for 15–30 minutes.

If using the roe, dust it lightly with flour. Heat remaining olive oil in a frying pan and fry roe until crisp. Scatter roe over scallops and serve with crusty bread or toast.

SERVES 4–6

Thai-style fish cakes with chilli dipping sauce

This great snack is totally moreish – just try and stop at one. Adjust the heat to your liking. I like a little heat to partner the intense burst of lime zing that comes from the lime leaves.

600 g rockling fillets or perch fillets, skin removed and pin-boned

2 eggs

3 tablespoons tom yum paste

1 stick lemongrass, white part only, finely shredded

2 teaspoons fish sauce

2 teaspoons castor sugar

1 red chilli, finely sliced

8 lime leaves, finely shredded

3 snake beans or 6 green beans, finely sliced

canola oil, for frying

chilli dipping sauce

100 ml water

2 teaspoons castor sugar

2 red chillies, finely sliced

3 teaspoons fish sauce

4 sprigs coriander, leaves picked

1 cucumber, peeled and chopped

2 red shallots, finely diced

Place fish fillets and eggs in a food processor and pulse to combine. Add tom yum paste, lemongrass, fish sauce, castor sugar and chilli and process until smooth and combined. Transfer to a bowl and mix in lime leaves and snake beans. Use your hands to shape mixture into small, flat rissoles about 5 cm in diameter.

To make the dipping sauce, warm water in a saucepan over medium heat. Add sugar and stir to dissolve. Remove from heat and add remaining ingredients. Set aside.

Deep fry fish cakes for 3–4 minutes in oil heated to 180°C in a deep fryer or heavy based saucepan. Drain on paper towel and serve immediately with dipping sauce. SERVES 6

> Tuna fritters with whipped fetta

Fond childhood memories of tuna patties made me rework the idea. Here, the classic tuna patty is given a facelift with spring onion, Tabasco and whipped fetta. Big and small kids will love these.

100 g fetta

100 g ricotta

50 ml pouring cream

185 g canned tuna in springwater, drained

2 teaspoons lemon zest

2 sprigs flat-leaf parsley, chopped

3 splashes Tabasco sauce

2 eggs

250 g potatoes, cooked and mashed

3 spring onions, sliced

3 cups (210 g) fresh breadcrumbs

½ cup (75 g) plain flour

olive oil, for frying

lemon wedges, to serve

watercress sprigs (optional), to serve

To make the whipped fetta, place fetta, ricotta and cream in a food processor with 3–4 tablespoons water and blend until smooth and light.

To make the fritters, place the tuna in a food processor and blend until smooth. Add lemon zest, parsley, Tabasco and 1 egg and process. Add potatoes and process until just combined. Transfer to a large bowl and mix in spring onions and 3 tablespoons breadcrumbs. Use your hands to shape mixture into small fritters about 6 cm in diameter.

Beat remaining egg. Dip fritters in flour to coat. Dip into beaten egg, then in remaining breadcrumbs. Heat olive oil in a large non-stick frying pan and fry fritters for 2 minutes on each side or until cooked, then drain on kitchen paper. Serve with whipped fetta, lemon wedges, and watercress if desired. SERVES 8–10

Prawns with iceberg, mint and garlic

When it comes to seafood, prawns are probably my favourite, and garlic prawns were often my choice in restaurants when I was growing up. So it's only natural to come up with a new, lighter, more interesting version of the classic. I've added crunchy iceberg lettuce to complement the creamy garlic sauce. That way, I can convince myself that it's just a salad.

10 thin slices baguette

50 ml olive oil, plus a little extra

salt flakes and freshly ground black pepper

1 small iceberg lettuce, finely shredded

4 sprigs mint, leaves picked and torn

4 spring onions, thinly sliced

24 green (raw) prawn cutlets, halved

3 cloves garlic, finely sliced

150 ml thickened or sour 'lite' cream

½ lemon, juiced

1 tablespoon butter

½ small bunch flat-leaf parsley leaves, chopped

Toast baguette or fry in a little olive oil. Season, then pulse in a food processor until coarsely crumbled.

Toss lettuce, mint and spring onions in a bowl. Heat olive oil in a non-stick frying pan over medium heat. Add prawn cutlets and cook for 1 minute. Add garlic, salt and pepper and cook for 2 minutes or until the prawns just change colour. Stir in cream, lemon juice, butter and parsley. Remove from heat. Arrange lettuce on a platter or individual plates, pour over prawn mixture and scatter with crumbled baguette. Serve immediately. SERVES 6

Prawn, fetta and watermelon salad

After having a fetta and watermelon salad in Greece, I decided to take this seemingly strange combination a step further and developed this stunning summer salad, adding prawns, chilli, sumac and generous amounts of fresh mint. It's wonderfully refreshing – cool but spicy, salty but with the sweetness of fresh prawns.

salt flakes and freshly ground black pepper

1 lemon, juiced, rind and flesh chopped

12 large green (raw) prawns, peeled with tails intact

100 ml extra virgin olive oil

2 small red chillies, finely sliced

3 teaspoons sumac (see glossary)

50 ml red-wine vinegar

3 golden shallots, sliced

3 spring onions, sliced

¼ seedless watermelon, cut into triangles

6 sprigs mint, leaves picked and torn

15 small sprigs flat-leaf parsley

125 g marinated goat's fetta, crumbled

squeeze of lemon juice, to serve

Heat a shallow frying pan of water over medium heat until boiling. Add ½ teaspoon salt, the chopped lemon and prawns and poach over low heat for 3–4 minutes or until prawns just change colour. Remove prawns and drain.

Combine olive oil, chilli, sumac, a splash of lemon juice, prawns, salt and pepper in a large bowl. Toss gently and set aside for 10 minutes.

Place vinegar and a pinch of salt in a small saucepan over medium heat and bring to the boil. Pour over golden shallots and set aside for 5 minutes. Drain, then add spring onions. Add onion mixture, watermelon, mint and parsley to prawn mixture.

Place prawns and watermelon on a platter, scatter with fetta, drizzle with any remaining oil and add a squeeze of lemon juice to taste. SERVES 4

Pan-fried garfish with soused cucumber People tend to steer clear of garfish because of the many bones, but I think they are missing out on a fantastic fish. Either choose very small garfish so the bones won't be an issue, or choose the largest so you can easily remove them. The sweetness and fine texture of garfish make it irresistible whether grilled, fried whole or filleted. The cucumber salad can be dressed and kept in the fridge for an hour before serving.

soused cucumber

4 Lebanese cucumbers

1 lemon, rind and flesh finely chopped

1 green chilli, finely sliced

1 tablespoon dill, finely chopped

3 sprigs tarragon, coarsely chopped

1 tablespoon sugar

½ cup (125 ml) extra virgin olive oil

1 tablespoon salt flakes

freshly ground black pepper

pan-fried garfish

8 small garfish, filleted, or
    4 large garfish to be fried whole

2 tablespoons plain flour

extra virgin olive oil, for frying

watercress sprigs (optional), to serve

To make the cucumber salad, peel the cucumbers to give a striped effect, then finely slice and place in a medium-sized bowl. Add remaining ingredients and toss gently to combine, then cover and set aside for 15 minutes.

Dip fish in flour to coat, and shake off excess. Heat olive oil in a frying pan over high heat and cook fish for 1½ minutes on each side or until just cooked through. Season with pepper. Spoon cucumber salad onto plates, top with the fish and scatter with watercress if desired. SERVES 4

Variation For something a little different, try the cucumber salad with pitted black olives and segmented blood oranges (or your favourite variety). Serve with a more robust fish, such as barramundi, hapuku or snapper, or chicken paillards (pan-fried or chargrilled flattened chicken breast slices). This combination is perfect in the cooler months.

Sardines wrapped in pancetta with sauce agro dolce

Give this recipe a go, even if you think you don't like sardines. The rich oily flesh of fresh sardines is well partnered with pancetta's salt-and-pork intensity, and the spicy but sweet tomato sauce marries these flavours perfectly.

⅓ cup (25 g) fresh breadcrumbs

1 clove garlic, finely chopped

1 sprig oregano, chopped

1 sprig flat-leaf parsley, chopped

8 sardine fillets, butterflied and boned
  (ask your fishmonger to do this)

salt flakes and freshly ground black pepper

8 slices pancetta

2–3 tablespoons olive oil

lemon wedges, to serve

sauce agro dolce

3 tablespoons olive oil

½ red onion, chopped

2 cloves garlic, chopped

1 small red chilli, finely chopped

2 red capsicums, roasted, peeled
  and coarsely chopped

1 × 400 g can crushed tomatoes

3 tablespoons red-wine vinegar

2 tablespoons castor sugar

salt flakes

To make the sauce agro dolce, heat olive oil in a saucepan over medium heat. Add onion, garlic and chilli and cook for 3 minutes or until onion is soft. Reduce heat to low. Add capsicum, tomatoes, vinegar, sugar and salt and cook, stirring, for 10 minutes or until mixture has a sauce-like consistency.

Place breadcrumbs, garlic, oregano and parsley in a small bowl and mix well. Season fish and sprinkle with breadcrumb mixture. Fold sardines in half lengthways and wrap in pancetta to seal.

Heat oil in a large frying pan over medium heat and cook sardines for 2–3 minutes on one side, turn carefully and cook for another 2–3 minutes, or until just cooked through. Spread the sauce agro dolce onto plates, place the sardines on top and serve with lemon wedges. Serve hot or warm. SERVES 4

Barbecued calamari, mint, lemon, chilli and couscous salad The idea for this salad came to me recently when I was on holiday. I returned from the fish co-op with a couple of kilos of super-fresh calamari but had limited pantry supplies at the house. This platter-style salad with its slightly random ingredients was the result.

Couscous is a magical golden grain that takes on any of the flavours it's teamed with. To prevent clumping, always add a splash of oil and rub the couscous in your hands before cooking.

500 g calamari tubes, cleaned

1½ cups (300 g) instant couscous

100 ml extra virgin olive oil

3 cloves garlic, finely sliced

2 small red chillies, sliced

2 spring onions, sliced

10 sprigs mint, leaves picked and torn

8 sprigs flat-leaf parsley, coarsely chopped

2 tablespoons gherkins, chopped

1 tablespoon capers, chopped

1 bunch asparagus, chargrilled for
  3–4 minutes and sliced

1 lime, juiced and zested

1 lemon, juiced and zested

salt flakes and freshly ground black pepper

3 tablespoons olive oil, extra

To prepare calamari, cut tubes into 4-cm sections. Flatten each section and make several horizontal slits, but not right to the ends, to give a ringed effect.

Place couscous in a large bowl, sprinkle with 2 tablespoons of the olive oil and add 500 ml boiling water. Stir, cover tightly with plastic film and set aside for 5 minutes.

Heat another 2 tablespoons of olive oil in a pan over low heat, then add garlic and chilli and cook for 2–4 minutes or until aromatic. Add garlic mixture to couscous and use a fork to stir and break up grains. Add spring onions, mint, parsley, gherkins, capers and asparagus and stir through.

To make citrus dressing, combine lime zest and juice and lemon zest and juice in a small bowl with remaining olive oil. Mix well and season.

Toss calamari in extra olive oil. Heat a chargrill or barbecue plate until hot, then grill calamari over high heat for 3–5 minutes, or until cooked and lightly coloured then transfer to a bowl. Pour citrus dressing over calamari, toss well and combine with couscous. Serve immediately. SERVES 4–6

Gherkins Add chopped gherkins to cooked lentils or rice to give an unexpected zing that brings out the flavours – both options match perfectly with fish or barbecued meats. You could also dress a lentil and pickle salad with herbs, olive oil and vinegar and serve it with a roast leg of lamb sprinkled with fetta.

Poached blue-eye with white zucchini, basil, chilli and mint salad

This dish can be served as a starter or light lunch with a generous dollop of mayonnaise and sliced crusty bread. It needs to be eaten and enjoyed straightaway or the zucchini will lose its crisp texture and the salad will be mushy.

1 lemon, juiced, rind and flesh chopped

salt flakes and freshly ground black pepper

2 × 220 g blue-eye fillets, with skin on

3 zucchini, white or pale green, coarsely grated

12 basil leaves, torn

4 sprigs mint, leaves picked and torn

2 green chillies, finely sliced

2 spring onions, finely sliced

½ cup (125 ml) extra virgin olive oil

1 lime, juiced

good quality mayonnaise and crusty bread (optional), to serve

Half-fill a deep frying pan with water. Bring water to the boil over high heat, then add chopped lemon and salt. Add fish fillets and poach for 5–7 minutes or until just cooked through. Drain and set aside, discarding lemon.

Place zucchini in a large bowl with basil, mint, chillies, spring onions and olive oil. Stir to combine and season. Flake fish into chunks and add to salad. Pour in lemon and lime juices and stir gently to combine. Serve immediately, with a dollop of mayonnaise and crusty bread. SERVES 4

White zucchini

White (or blonde) zucchini are in season from around May to December and have a sensational sweet flavour. You don't need to cook them – raw zucchini, grated coarsely, is delicious dressed with lemon juice, olive oil and salt and pepper, and can be added to almost any green salad. Another option is to stir grated zucchini through hot pasta at the last minute along with ricotta, lemon juice, salt and pepper.

Poached blue-eye with harissa, sumac and lime couscous

This quick and simple salad-style dish uses the delicious spice sumac. Harissa can be toned down to your liking. Just use less of the fiery paste and add more lime to the couscous to accompany it.

650 g blue-eye fillet, pin-boned
   and cut into 3 pieces

salt flakes

25 ml extra virgin olive oil

4 golden shallots, peeled, halved and sliced

3 cloves garlic, sliced

1 large red chilli, finely sliced

4 tablespoons fresh harissa (see glossary)

2 teaspoons sumac (see glossary)

2 teaspoons brown sugar

6 sprigs mint, leaves picked and torn

6 sprigs coriander, leaves picked and torn

mint leaves and coriander leaves, extra, to serve

lime couscous

1 cup (200 g) couscous

25 ml extra virgin olive oil

2 cups (500 ml) boiling water

1 lime, juiced and zested

2 tablespoons slivered almonds

To make lime couscous, place couscous and olive oil in a medium-sized bowl and rub together to coat the grains. Pour over boiling water, stir and cover with plastic film. Set aside for 5 minutes. Add lime zest and juice and almonds and stir with a fork to break up grains.

Half-fill a deep frying pan with water. Bring water to the boil over high heat. Add fish pieces and poach for 6 minutes or until just cooked through. Drain and set aside.

To make the dressing, heat olive oil in a small frying pan over medium heat. Add golden shallots, garlic and chilli and cook until shallots are soft. Season with salt. Spoon into a large bowl. Add harissa, sumac, sugar, mint and coriander and mix well. Flake the fish into chunks, place in bowl and mix gently with the dressing.

To serve, pile couscous onto a platter or plates, top with the fish and scatter with extra mint and coriander. SERVES 4

Octopus with oregano and vinegar

You can't go wrong with this braised octopus. It's beautifully tender and a terrific addition to an antipasto platter. Don't be scared of heating up an empty pot and just dropping the octopus in – it won't burn because the juices will be released almost immediately. Note that the recipe needs no salt, as octopus is naturally salty.

1.5 kg large octopus tentacles, divided into singles

1 bay leaf

2 cloves garlic, peeled

100 ml white-wine vinegar

150 ml extra virgin olive oil

freshly ground black pepper

3–4 sprigs oregano, leaves picked and chopped

150 g fetta, sliced (optional)

Heat a large heavy-based saucepan over high heat. When it is very hot, add octopus legs and bay leaf, cover and cook for 20–25 minutes or until the octopus is tender and juices are released. Remove octopus and bay leaf, and reserve juices. Place half the juices, garlic, vinegar, olive oil and pepper in a food processor or blender and process until smooth. Stir in chopped oregano.

Cut octopus into small pieces, place in a bowl and pour dressing over. Toss gently to combine. Serve warm over slivers of fetta or as part of an antipasto platter.

If you have some octopus left over, warm it through in a non-stick frying pan and serve with a splash of fresh vinegar. SERVES 8–10

Octopus It is worth making this recipe in a larger batch, as the octopus cooks more evenly in the pot. Once you know how to do it, you'll never have to buy commercially pickled octopus again.

Fried spiced quail with eggplant paste and date, chilli and blood orange salad

This is my 'left of field' Greek version of spicy fried quail. It makes a delicious starter. Yummy.

eggplant paste

2 large eggplants

100 ml extra virgin olive oil

⅓ cup (95 g) plain Greek-style yoghurt

1 tablespoon lemon juice

2 pinches salt flakes

spiced quail

1 tablespoon ground cumin

1 tablespoon ground fennel seeds

1 tablespoon ground cinnamon

2 teaspoons ground coriander

2 teaspoons ground chilli flakes

1 tablespoon salt flakes

freshly ground black pepper, to taste

1 cup (150 g) plain flour

4 jumbo quails, halved with backbone removed (see note)

vegetable oil, for frying

blood orange salad

½ bunch coriander, leaves picked

½ bunch mint, leaves picked

4 fresh dates, seeded and quartered

1 large green or red chilli, seeded and sliced

2 blood oranges, 1 juiced and 1 cut into segments

⅓ cup (80 ml) extra virgin olive oil

½ lemon, juiced

Preheat oven to 170°C. To make eggplant paste, cut eggplants in half lengthways, score flesh and drizzle with olive oil. Bake on a lightly greased baking tray for about 25 minutes or until golden and cooked. When cool enough to handle, remove flesh and chop very finely. Place in a bowl, then stir in yoghurt, lemon juice and salt. Cover and set aside at room temperature.

To prepare the quail, place spices, salt, pepper and flour in a shallow bowl or plastic bag and combine well. Pat quail dry with kitchen paper, dip into spice mix, then shake off excess. Fry quail in a deep fryer at 180°C for 4–5 minutes or until golden and cooked. (Or you can deep-fry quail in hot vegetable oil in a large saucepan.) Drain on kitchen paper.

To make the blood orange salad, combine coriander leaves, mint leaves, dates and chilli in a medium bowl. Place blood orange juice, olive oil and lemon juice in a small bowl and whisk. Pour about a third of the dressing over salad and toss to combine.

To serve, spoon eggplant paste onto four plates, place quail on top, then pile salad onto quail. Drizzle remaining dressing around quail and scatter with blood orange segments. SERVES 4

Butterflying quail Ask your butcher to remove the backbones of the quails. To prepare the quails for frying, tip the spice mix into a plastic bag. Place quails in the bag, then shake until evenly coated.

Michael's baked cannellini beans with chorizo, egg and fetta

My partner makes this dish and it's a bona-fide hangover fix! You could also be a bit more sophisticated and serve it with a bitter green salad dressed with wine vinegar and extra virgin olive oil, and a glass of wine, for a brunch or lunch. Either way, some toasted sourdough is a must.

olive oil, for cooking

8 cm spicy chorizo sausage, diced

3 golden shallots, finely sliced

4 cloves garlic, finely chopped

4 sprigs oregano, torn

1 bay leaf

2 × 400 g cans cannellini beans, drained and rinsed

⅓ cup (80 ml) red-wine vinegar

4 tablespoons tomato paste

1 × 400 g can crushed tomatoes

salt flakes and freshly ground black pepper

4 free-range eggs

150 g fetta

50 ml extra virgin olive oil

toasted sourdough fingers, to serve

Heat a little oil in a heavy-based saucepan over medium heat, add chorizo and fry for 3–5 minutes. Add shallots, garlic, oregano and bay leaf and cook, stirring occasionally, for 5 minutes. Stir in beans, vinegar, tomato paste, tomatoes and 2–3 tablespoons water and simmer for about 15 minutes or until thick. Season to taste.

Preheat oven to 170°C. Pour mixture into a medium (1.5-litre capacity) ovenproof dish. Use the back of a spoon to make 4 holes in mixture. Crack eggs into holes.

Crumble fetta over the top, drizzle with olive oil and bake in the preheated oven for 10–15 minutes or until eggs are cooked but still runny. Serve with toasted sourdough fingers on the side. SERVES 4

Chow-mein-style beef with cabbage, peas and vermicelli

This dish can be enjoyed for a casual Sunday-night dinner with a DVD, or prepared to take to work the next day – it just needs a quick reheat. If serving as a sit-down meal or as part of a banquet, fry extra noodles in vegetable oil until crispy and sprinkle on top.

3 tablespoons olive oil

400 g beef mince

2 pinches Chinese five-spice powder

2 pinches chilli powder (optional)

1 large brown onion, sliced

4 cloves garlic, finely chopped

50 g fresh ginger, grated

¼ cabbage, finely sliced

1½ tablespoons oyster sauce

100 ml tamari (see glossary)

2–3 teaspoons sesame oil

½ cup frozen peas

4 spring onions, sliced diagonally

3 green chillies, sliced

100 g vermicelli (thin rice noodles),
   cooked in boiling water for 1½ minutes

salt flakes and freshly ground black pepper

Heat oil in a large wok over very high heat. Add beef and cook, stirring to break up, for 3–5 minutes or until well browned. Sprinkle in five-spice powder and chilli powder, if using.

Add onion, garlic and ginger and stir. Add sliced cabbage and 125 ml hot water and stir again. Stir in oyster sauce, tamari and sesame oil. Add peas, spring onions, chillies and noodles. Stir, then, if needed, add a splash more hot water. Check seasoning and serve immediately. SERVES 4

> Spiedini of bacon, bocconcini and bread with roasted tomatoes

I adore these for a funky breakfast if there's time to go to a little extra trouble. If you have fresh bay leaves, they are great threaded next to the bacon pieces on the skewers, adding a wonderful smoky flavour.

8 small or 4 medium vine-ripened tomatoes

100 ml extra virgin olive oil

½ cup oregano leaves

½ loaf sourdough bread,
   cut into 2 cm cubes

8 rashers rindless bacon, halved

12 bocconcini, halved

freshly ground black pepper

Preheat oven to 200°C. Score tomatoes in a circle around the middle, and place on a baking tray. Drizzle half the olive oil over tomatoes, then scatter with oregano leaves. Roast for 15–20 minutes. Set aside to rest for 5 minutes.

Thread bread, bacon and bocconcini on 8 × 15–20 cm metal or wooden skewers, starting and finishing with a bread cube. Drizzle the remaining olive oil over the skewers and season with pepper.

Preheat a barbecue, cast-iron chargrill pan or grill. When hot, cook skewers for 1–2 minutes, turning occasionally, until the bread is toasted. Serve with roasted tomatoes on the side. SERVES 4

Crumbed zucchini flowers with crab, mayonnaise and peas

At first the focus is on the zucchini flowers, but then you'll taste the luscious crab mayo and be longing for more. Look for zucchini flowers with baby zucchini attached: these are female zucchini flowers – male flowers are blooms and stems only.

8 zucchini flowers with zucchini attached

2 cups (140 g) soft white breadcrumbs (see note)

salt flakes and freshly ground black pepper

1 handful flat-leaf parsley leaves, finely chopped

2 lemons, finely zested

½ cup (75 g) plain flour

2 eggs, beaten with 1 tablespoon water

1 tablespoon extra virgin olive oil

1 spring onion, finely chopped

1 clove garlic, finely chopped

200 g fresh cooked crabmeat, from your fishmonger

¾ cup (200 g) mayonnaise

½ cup (125 ml) pouring cream, whipped

2 tablespoons plain yoghurt

2 teaspoons lemon juice

2 cups (500 ml) canola oil

½ cup fresh or frozen peas, blanched, then tossed with a little extra virgin olive oil

½ bunch chives, finely chopped

½ bunch chervil sprigs

lemon wedges, to serve

Trim zucchini flowers (leaving zucchini attached) and remove style from inside flowers. Slice zucchini halfway up to allow even cooking. Place breadcrumbs, salt, pepper, parsley and lemon zest in a shallow bowl and stir to combine. Dip zucchini flowers in flour and shake lightly to remove excess. Dip in beaten egg and shake to remove excess. Roll gently in breadcrumb mixture to coat, then set aside for 10 minutes.

Place olive oil, spring onion and garlic in a small saucepan over low heat and cook until onion is translucent. Stir through crabmeat to just warm it. Remove from heat and set aside to cool. In a medium bowl, stir together the mayonnaise, whipped cream, yoghurt and lemon juice. Add crabmeat mixture, season to taste and stir to combine.

Heat canola oil in a large saucepan over medium heat until hot (175°C). Deep-fry zucchini for 3–4 minutes or until golden and cooked. Drain on kitchen paper.

To serve, place a generous scoop of mayonnaise on four plates, top each with zucchinis, scatter over peas and herbs and add a lemon wedge. SERVES 4

Breadcrumbs To make soft crumbs, you need day-old sliced white bread, torn up and pulse-blended in a food processor until you have rough crumbs. Combine with lemon rind, oregano and grated parmesan and you have the perfect mix to crumb chicken or veal schnitzel for a simple midweek meal.

Saganaki with cucumber, spring onion and green chilli salad

One hot summer afternoon I had guests drop in and I pulled this dish together from what I had on hand. In less than 20 minutes I was joining my friends for a cold glass of soave. Saganaki means 'shallow-fried cheese'. I've used kefalograviera, which is available from good delis, but you can also use haloumi. The sesame and cheese combination is just sensational.

2 Lebanese cucumbers

3 spring onions, sliced diagonally

3 sprigs mint, leaves picked and torn

1 green chilli, sliced

1 lemon, juiced

salt flakes and freshly ground black pepper

3 tablespoons plain flour

3 tablespoons sesame seeds

4 slices kefalograviera cheese (see glossary)

150 ml olive oil

1 lemon, thickly sliced

crusty bread, to serve

Peel the cucumbers to give a striped effect and thinly slice lengthways into ribbons. Combine with spring onions, mint, chilli and lemon juice in a medium bowl. Season lightly.

Mix flour and seeds together in a bowl. Lightly dampen cheese slices in water, then dip into sesame seed mixture to coat. Heat oil in a frying pan over medium heat. Add cheese and fry on each side for 2–3 minutes or until golden. Remove and drain well on kitchen paper.

Serve immediately with cucumber salad, lemon slices and crusty bread.

SERVES 4

Spinach, herb, ricotta and fetta filo pastry pie

This pie was inspired by my mother-in-law's traditional Macedonian musznik, but essentially it is a spanakopita. It's a yummy snack and great for picnics. You can eat it cold and serve it with tzatziki, if you wish. Use standard filo or hunt for a homemade version, sometimes available from delis and Lebanese specialty shops.

150 ml extra virgin olive oil

1 brown onion, chopped

3 cloves garlic, finely chopped

2 tablespoons capers, chopped

800–900 g spinach (with stems), coarsely chopped

4 sprigs mint, leaves picked and torn

4 sprigs oregano, leaves picked and torn

4 sprigs flat-leaf parsley, leaves picked and torn

2 eggs, lightly beaten

250 g ricotta

120 g fetta, crumbled

salt flakes and freshly ground black pepper

12 large sheets filo pastry

2 teaspoons ground fennel seeds

Heat 50 ml of the olive oil in a large, heavy-based saucepan over medium heat. Add onion and garlic and cook for 2–3 minutes. Add capers and half the spinach and cook for 4–5 minutes. Drain in a colander and press out excess liquid. Transfer to a bowl and set aside.

Add a little more oil to the pan and cook herbs and remaining spinach until wilted. Drain in a colander and press out excess liquid. Add to bowl. Stir eggs, ricotta and fetta into spinach mixture and mix well. Season.

Preheat oven to 165°C.

Grease a round 20 cm cake tin and line the base with baking paper. Keep the filo covered with a damp tea towel while working so it doesn't dry out. Place two pastry sheets on a lightly floured surface and brush with olive oil. Repeat twice more. Place half the spinach mixture along the centre of pastry and roll lengthways. Place roll in a circle around the inside rim of the cake tin. Make another roll with remaining pastry and spinach mixture. Place in cake tin and wind around to completely cover base of tin. Brush with olive oil, scatter with fennel seeds, and salt and pepper. Bake for 30–40 minutes or until golden. Cool before serving. SERVES 6

Sautéed cepe and pine mushrooms on taleggio bruschetta

This is a delicious light lunch or a fantastic starter to an autumn meal. It's very easy and quick because it's all in the quality of the ingredients. The type of mushrooms can be substituted with your old favourites if the varieties below are not available, but definitely take the time to source the taleggio.

4 thick slices crusty bread

4 slices taleggio cheese (see glossary)

30 ml extra virgin olive oil

100 g butter, chopped

4 cepe or slippery jack mushrooms,
   trimmed and sliced

4 pine mushrooms, trimmed and sliced

1 clove garlic, finely sliced

salt flakes and freshly ground black pepper

½ lemon, juiced

4 sprigs flat-leaf parsley, leaves picked and torn

Toast bread, then top with taleggio. Put toast slices under a hot grill for 2 minutes or until melted. Combine olive oil and half the butter in a frying pan over medium heat. When butter is melted, add mushrooms and garlic. Season with salt and pepper. Cook, tossing mushrooms frequently, for about 3 minutes or until softened. Add lemon juice, remaining butter and parsley. Check seasoning. To serve, spoon mushrooms over bruschetta. SERVES 4

Braised artichokes with almonds, white wine and soft-boiled eggs

I like to serve this salad for a light winter lunch, but it could also be a starter at a larger affair. Once the artichokes are braised, they can be kept in their own liquid for a couple of days and used in other dishes. One option is to warm them through, add peas and parsley and serve with grilled chicken, veal or lamb.

200 ml extra virgin olive oil

4 large fresh artichokes, prepared
   (see note) and quartered

salt flakes and freshly ground black pepper

2 cloves garlic, finely chopped

2 sprigs thyme

1 bay leaf

½ lemon, juiced

200 ml white wine

1 bunch watercress, sprigs picked

¾ cup (100 g) slivered almonds, toasted

3 free-range eggs, soft-boiled

100 g fromage frais (see glossary)

80 g Ligurian olives

crusty bread, to serve

Heat olive oil in a wide, heavy-based saucepan over medium heat. Add artichokes, salt and pepper and cook, stirring occasionally, for about 5 minutes or until slightly coloured. Stir in garlic, thyme and bay leaf. Add lemon juice, wine and a splash of water. Simmer for about 15 minutes or until artichokes are tender. Cool for 15 minutes, then drain, reserving cooking liquid.

Scatter half the watercress over a serving plate, add drained artichokes and sprinkle with almonds. Break over soft-boiled eggs, add a scoop of fromage frais and olives. Scatter with remaining watercress, season lightly and drizzle over reserved cooking juices. Serve with crusty bread. SERVES 4

To prepare artichokes Remove at least 20–30 outer leaves until you see light yellow flesh. Trim off the top 5 cm. Trim the stalk to about 5 cm in length and pare away the outer skin to reveal the light-green inner flesh. You should end up with a thick disk attached to a slender stem. Rub the entire surface of the artichoke with lemon juice.

Eggplant involtini with ricotta, mozzarella and tomato

This traditional southern Italian dish makes an excellent accompaniment for grilled meat or a mixed-leaf salad dressed with balsamic vinegar and extra virgin olive oil.

3 eggs

2 large eggplants

½ cup (75 g) plain flour

300 ml olive oil, for frying

250 g ricotta

salt flakes and freshly ground black pepper

3 tablespoons currants, soaked in red-wine vinegar for 5 minutes, then drained

½ cup (40 g) grated parmesan

200 g mozzarella, cut into 1 cm-thick sticks

½ cup (125 ml) extra virgin olive oil

2 cups (500 ml) tomato passata

2 sprigs flat-leaf parsley, chopped

50 g pine nuts, coarsely chopped

3 tablespoons coarse breadcrumbs

In a small bowl, lightly beat 2 eggs with 1 tablespoon water. Peel the eggplants to create a striped effect, then cut lengthways into 1 cm-thick slices. Dust the eggplant slices with flour, then dip in egg wash. Heat olive oil in a large heavy-based frying pan over high heat. Cook eggplant slices for 1–2 minutes on each side or until golden. Drain well on kitchen paper.

In a medium bowl, mix ricotta with remaining egg. Season with salt and pepper. Add the drained currants and half the parmesan and stir to combine. Spoon about 1 tablespoon of the ricotta mixture onto each eggplant slice. Add a stick of mozzarella and roll up tightly.

Preheat oven to 170°C. Brush the base of a large ovenproof dish with 1 tablespoon of the extra virgin olive oil. Spread half the tomato passata in base of dish. Place the eggplant rolls on the tomato passata, seam-side down so they don't unroll. Drizzle with remaining olive oil, spoon over remaining passata and sprinkle with remaining parmesan.

Combine parsley, pine nuts and breadcrumbs in a small bowl. Sprinkle over top. Cover with foil and bake for 25 minutes. Remove foil and bake for a further 10 minutes or until cheese is melted and gooey. SERVES 6

Provençale capsicums These slow-roasted capsicums are served with a filling of cherry tomatoes, anchovies, olives and breadcrumbs – a fantastic combination.

2 punnets (500 g) cherry tomatoes, halved

5 tablespoons black olives, pitted and finely chopped

4 sprigs oregano, torn

4 sprigs flat-leaf parsley, chopped

2 cloves garlic, finely chopped

salt flakes and freshly ground black pepper

4 red capsicums, halved and seeded

¾ cup (55 g) homemade breadcrumbs

½ cup (125 ml) extra virgin olive oil

8 anchovy fillets, sliced lengthways

Preheat oven to 150°C. Combine tomatoes, olives, herbs and garlic in a medium bowl. Season with salt and pepper. Place capsicum halves on a lightly greased baking tray and fill with tomato mixture. Sprinkle with breadcrumbs and drizzle with olive oil. Place anchovies on top in a crisscross pattern. Cover with foil and bake for 35 minutes, then remove foil and bake for another 25 minutes until soft and golden. Serve with pan juices poured over. SERVES 4–8

Variations Provençale capsicums can be turned into a light lunch with a green salad and wedges of goat's cheese. Or if you have leftovers and want a quick dinner, peel off and discard the capsicum skin and roughly chop the flesh. Stir, along with the sauce, through cooked short pasta with parmesan and garlic. You could also add fresh or canned tuna.

> Fried egg with hummus, red onion and sumac salad This is my personal breakfast favourite and I often enjoy it. It's super-easy to prepare, and if making your own hummus is too much trouble, buy it from the supermarket or deli.

½ cup (125 ml) extra virgin olive oil

1 lemon, juiced

1 × 400 g can chickpeas, drained

2 tablespoons tahini

salt flakes and freshly ground black pepper

½ red onion, finely sliced

1 cup flat-leaf parsley leaves, coarsely chopped

1 tablespoon sumac (see glosasry)

4 free-range eggs

4 slices sourdough bread, toasted, rubbed lightly
    with 1 clove garlic and drizzled with olive oil

To make the salad dressing, place 2 tablespoons olive oil with half the lemon juice in a small bowl. Mix well, then set aside.

To make hummus, place chickpeas in a medium saucepan, cover with water and bring to the boil over medium heat. Remove and drain. Place in the bowl of a food processor and add remaining olive oil and lemon juice, tahini, salt and pepper. Process until it is a smooth paste.

To make the red onion salad, place onion, parsley, half the sumac and dressing in a small bowl and toss to combine.

Fry eggs sunny-side up in a lightly greased non-stick frying pan. Spread hummus over toast and top each slice with an egg. Top with onion salad, sprinkle with remaining sumac and season to taste. SERVES 4

Gorgonzola pannacotta with salad of apple, radicchio, walnuts and balsamic

Savoury pannacotta is unusual but delicious, a modern take on a great classic. As an alternative to individual serves, set it in a loaf tin and slice into easy-to-serve rectangles like I have here. This pannacotta is simple and fresh – great for an entrée or a light lunch, or take it to a party and serve the salad alongside.

1 head radicchio, leaves torn

4 sticks celery, sliced

2 granny smith apples, cored and cut into fine strips

20 basil leaves

½ cup (50 g) walnuts, toasted and chopped

½ cup (125 ml) extra virgin olive oil

3 tablespoons balsamic vinegar

pannacotta

3 leaves gelatine (gold strength,
    see glossary)

1 cup (250 ml) milk

150 ml pouring cream

140 g gorgonzola piccante (see glossary),
    rind removed and finely chopped

salt flakes and freshly ground black pepper

Place gelatine in a small bowl of cold water and soak until soft. Combine milk and cream in a small saucepan, place over medium heat and bring to a simmer. Remove from heat and gently whisk in gorgonzola. Season. Squeeze water from gelatine. Add gelatine leaves to milk mixture and stir until dissolved. Strain and pour into 4 × 100 ml moulds or a loaf tin. Cover and refrigerate for 6 hours or until set.

To make the salad, combine all ingredients except oil and vinegar in a large bowl. Place oil and vinegar in a small bowl, whisk until smooth and pour over salad. Toss gently to combine.

To serve, unmould pannacotta (by dipping the moulds in warm water for a few seconds); if set in a loaf tin, slice into 2 cm-thick rectangles. Place on serving plates with salad on top. SERVES 4

Baked figs with walnut cream and tarragon salad

When buying figs, always look for the heaviest or slightly split ones as they are the ripest and are ready to eat. Lightweight figs don't ripen well as they have not had enough water when growing, and will have little flavour.

8 ripe figs

150 g mascarpone

1½ cups (150 g) walnuts, toasted

salt flakes and freshly ground black pepper

½ lemon

½ bunch watercress, sprigs picked

100 g wild rocket leaves

5 sprigs French tarragon, leaves picked

100 ml extra virgin olive oil

100 ml vincotto (see glossary)
   or aged balsamic vinegar

Preheat oven to 170°C. Cut the figs almost into quarters, so that they are open but still in one piece. Place mascarpone in a small bowl with 1 tablespoon cold water and whisk until it has the consistency of thick cream. Pulse 100 g of the walnuts in a food processor until finely chopped. Add to mascarpone and stir to combine. Season.

Squeeze a little lemon juice over the figs, then spoon a dollop of mascarpone mixture on each fig. Place figs on a baking tray lined with baking paper and bake for 8–10 minutes.

Place watercress, rocket and tarragon leaves in a bowl. Add remaining lemon juice and olive oil and toss to combine. Serve figs with watercress salad and scatter with remaining walnuts. Drizzle with vincotto or balsamic vinegar. SERVES 4

Green chilli and scrambled eggs with asparagus and parmesan

Green chilli and scrambled eggs with asparagus and parmesan When it is in season, white asparagus can be used in place of green, or a bunch of each looks beautiful. I tend to only use asparagus when it is in season (around spring to summer), as the flavour and quality then is truly superior.

1 cup mint leaves

1 cup flat-leaf parsley leaves

1 cup coriander leaves

2 tablespoons capers

3 long green chillies, seeded and
    sliced diagonally

3 spring onions, sliced diagonally

Tabasco sauce, to taste

50 ml extra virgin olive oil

100 g shaved pecorino (see glossary)
    or parmesan

2 bunches asparagus, trimmed

salt flakes and freshly ground black pepper

6 free-range eggs

1 tablespoon extra virgin olive oil, extra

buttered toast (optional), to serve

Combine mint, parsley, coriander and capers and coarsely chop. Place in a medium-sized bowl with chillies and spring onions. Add Tabasco to taste, then stir in 1 tablespoon olive oil and half the cheese.

Cook asparagus in lightly salted boiling water for about 3 minutes. Drain, season to taste and set aside.

Whisk eggs until frothy. Heat a non-stick frying pan over high heat and add remaining olive oil. Pour in eggs and cook over a low heat, stirring with a fork, for 2–3 minutes or until eggs are almost cooked but still creamy. Add eggs to herb mixture and toss gently to combine.

Place asparagus spears on serving plates and top with scrambled eggs and herbs. Sprinkle with remaining cheese and drizzle over the extra olive oil. Serve with hot, buttered toast on the side, if desired. SERVES 4

Mozzarella en carrozza

Mozzarella en carrozza For another delicious brunch idea, cut your favourite sourdough baguette into 1-centimetre slices. Sandwich a slice of fresh mozzarella between slices of baguette. Coat both sides of the sandwich in flour, then dip in beaten egg. Shallow-fry in extra virgin olive oil until golden. Sprinkle with salt flakes and serve immediately – it's to die for!

Middles

Drawn from both my heritage and my experience, my cooking has a strong Mediterranean influence; Italy, of course, but north Africa and Greece, too, and I think it shows in the following recipes.

Many are dishes one might expect in a village as much as a city: braised rabbit, chicken and oxtail; slow-roasted duck and pork dishes; seafood stew; roasted snapper; osso bucco; a seafood pie.

Most dishes can be plated in a more formal fashion, but I recommend placing them on the table and serving from the pot. By all means serve and portion the food yourself, but doing it in front of your family or guests is far more intimate and connected, and emphasises the wonderful feelings of community and welcome that shared food evokes.

Taking it slowly is another important element in several of the following dishes. Don't be put off by this, embrace it. Slow-cooked food doesn't take up your time; it just takes a little planning and, with experience, only occasional attention. Let the flavours develop, giving them depth and nuance, and cook ample quantities, allowing plenty to share and enough for leftovers.

Roman pork sausage ragu

You can serve this beautiful ragu with any kind of pasta. One Sunday when Michael and I were craving lasagne, I added two extra cans of tomatoes to this recipe then stirred through some fresh mozzarella, basil and parmesan – it was delicious.

250 g pork and veal sausages

150 ml extra virgin olive oil

80 g pancetta (see glossary), chopped

1 bay leaf

3 sprigs rosemary, leaves removed from stem

1 tablespoon ground aniseed

2 sprigs thyme

5 cloves garlic, finely chopped

2 small red chillies, finely sliced

1 medium carrot, chopped

1½ brown onions, chopped

3 sticks celery, finely sliced

2 tablespoons tomato paste

3 cups (750 ml) red wine

2½ cups (625 ml) water

1 × 400 g can peeled tomatoes, crushed

salt flakes and freshly ground black pepper

500 g dried pappardelle or other ribbon pasta

parmigiano reggiano, to serve

Skin sausages and crumble meat. Heat a large heavy-based saucepan over medium heat. Cook sausage meat, stirring occasionally, for 6–10 minutes or until golden brown. Add 100 ml of the oil, then add pancetta, bay leaf, rosemary, aniseed and thyme and stir. Add garlic, chillies, carrot, onion and celery and stir well. Cook over a low-medium heat for 10 minutes or until onion is soft and caramelised. Stir in tomato paste. Pour in wine and bring to a simmer. Add water and tomatoes and simmer over medium heat, partially covered, for 30–45 minutes or until sauce thickens and oil floats to the top. Check seasoning.

Bring a large saucepan of lightly salted water to the boil. Add pasta and cook until al dente. Drain.

Stir ragu through the hot pasta. Serve immediately, drizzled with remaining oil and a sprinkle of freshly grated parmigiano. SERVES 4

Wild mushroom ragu on wet polenta with mascarpone

On a cold night, this dish can replace the standard meat stew. It's hearty and warms the soul. Promise.

⅓ cup (80 ml) extra virgin olive oil

100 g butter, chopped

4 golden shallots, sliced

2 cloves garlic, finely sliced

salt flakes and freshly ground black pepper

1 bay leaf

3 sprigs thyme

10 g dried porcini mushrooms,
  soaked in hot water, drained and chopped

250 g field mushrooms, chopped

50 g enoki mushrooms

250 g cepe mushrooms, trimmed and sliced

250 g pine mushrooms, trimmed and sliced

100 ml white wine

300 ml chicken stock

1 cup instant polenta

150 g grated parmesan, plus extra to serve

100 g mascarpone

Heat olive oil and half the butter in a large frying pan over high heat. Add golden shallots and garlic, season with salt and pepper, then fry gently. Add bay leaf and thyme and cook over medium heat for 5 minutes. Add all the mushrooms, then pour in wine and stir. Add stock and simmer for 15 minutes.

Bring 1 litre of water to the boil in a large saucepan, then reduce to low-medium heat. Rain in the polenta, whisking constantly for 10–15 minutes or until polenta is thick and cooked. Add parmesan and remaining butter, stir through and season.

To serve, spoon polenta into bowls and make a well. Spoon mushrooms into well and add a dollop of mascarpone. Pass around extra parmesan separately. SERVES 6

Braised duck ragu with verjuice and lasagnoni

This is a gorgeous pasta sauce. I like to serve it with lasagnoni or gnocchi but you could try it with your favourite short pasta or mash. Roasting the duck first renders the fat, and gives good colour to the finished ragu.

1 × size 24 duck, neck removed and cavity trimmed of fat, cut into quarters

salt flakes and freshly ground black pepper

3 tablespoons extra virgin olive oil

1 brown onion, finely chopped

6 cloves garlic, finely sliced

1 fresh bay leaf

1 celeriac, peeled and finely chopped

2 leeks, finely sliced

2 medium carrots, finely chopped

5 sprigs thyme

600 ml verjuice (see glossary)

3 litres good-quality chicken stock

chopped flat-leaf parsley (optional), to serve

500 g dried lasagnoni (short flat ribbons) or similar

grated parmesan, to serve

Preheat oven to 200°C. Season duck with salt and pepper. Place on a roasting rack in a baking dish and roast on top shelf of oven for 35 minutes or until golden.

Heat oil in a very large, heavy-based saucepan over medium heat. Add onion, garlic, bay leaf, salt and pepper and stir. Stir in celeriac, leek and carrot. Cook for 15 minutes or until vegetables are tender. Add thyme, duck and verjuice and simmer for 5 minutes. Add stock and simmer for 40 minutes or until duck is very tender. Remove duck and while it is still warm, use your fingers or a knife to remove skin and meat from the bones. Slice the meat evenly and return to sauce. Boil over high heat, stirring regularly, for 5–10 minutes or until sauce is reduced and thickened. Season well and add parsley, if using.

Bring a large saucepan of lightly salted water to the boil. Add pasta and cook until al dente. Drain. Stir duck and sauce through pasta and serve sprinkled with parmesan.
SERVES 4

Using duck fat

Duck fat is great for roasting potatoes. After roasting a duck, drain fat and freeze it to use at a later stage. All you do then is melt the fat in a baking tray and toss in peeled, parboiled potatoes, salt and pepper, a couple of smashed garlic cloves, bay leaf, thyme or rosemary and roast at 200°C till crispy and crunchy. Deliciously addictive.

Pappardelle with confit of mushrooms, asparagus, thyme and butter

I love mushrooms. For the mixed selection, choose at least three different types. Try Swiss brown, shiitake, portobello, enoki, abalone, black and white fungus or button.

⅔ cup (160 ml) extra virgin olive oil

3 spring onions, finely chopped

4 cloves garlic, finely sliced

6–8 sprigs thyme

1 bay leaf

100 g field mushrooms, stalks trimmed, peeled and coarsely chopped

50 g dried porcini mushrooms, soaked in boiling water briefly, then drained

700 g mixed mushrooms

100 g butter, chopped

1 cup (250 ml) white wine

salt flakes and freshly ground black pepper

500 g fresh pappardelle

1 bunch asparagus, trimmed and cut into 2 cm lengths

1 cup flat-leaf parsley leaves, torn

extra olive oil (optional)

120 g shaved parmesan, to serve

Heat olive oil in a large heavy-based saucepan over medium heat. Add spring onions, garlic, thyme and bay leaf and cook for 4 minutes. Add field mushrooms and porcini and stir well. Coarsely chop large mixed mushrooms and slice small mushrooms. Add to pan with butter and white wine. Season with salt and pepper. Reduce heat to low and simmer for 10–15 minutes.

Bring a large saucepan of lightly salted water to the boil. Add pasta and cook for 4–6 minutes or until al dente. Drain.

Meanwhile, cook asparagus in lightly salted boiling water for 3 minutes. Drain.

Add asparagus to mushroom mixture and warm through over low heat. Add pasta and parsley to mushrooms, stir. Add extra olive oil if desired. Serve immediately, with shaved parmesan scattered on top. SERVES 4

Pennette with prawns, broccolini and mascarpone

Pennette pasta is so cute, and pairing it with prawns and lemon is very Italian. The broccolini must be well cooked for this dish to work, and make sure you use mascarpone rather than regular cream – it's much more intense and has a pleasant tang.

500 g dried pennette

2 bunches broccolini, chopped into ½ cm lengths

150 ml extra virgin olive oil

12 green (raw) prawns, peeled and chopped into very small pieces

salt flakes and freshly ground black pepper

3 large cloves garlic, finely chopped

3 red chillies, finely chopped

½ bunch parsley leaves, roughly sliced

100 ml white wine

1 lemon, juiced and zested

4 tablespoons mascarpone

Bring a large saucepan of lightly salted water to the boil. Add pasta and cook for 3 minutes, then add broccolini and cook for 6 more minutes.

Meanwhile, heat half the oil in a large frying pan over high heat. Add prawns, season with salt and pepper, and cook, stirring constantly, for 3 minutes. Add garlic and chilli and cook for 2 minutes. Add parsley and cook for 1 more minute, then add wine and lemon juice and zest and remove from heat.

Drain pasta and return to saucepan. Pour prawn mixture over pasta and toss to coat. Add mascarpone, check seasoning and add extra lemon juice if needed. Serve immediately. SERVES 4

> Tagliatelle alla norma

Throw the eggplant in the oven, pour yourself a glass of wine and dinner is almost sorted. This pasta dish is the perfect midweek meal.

2 eggplants, halved and flesh scored

½ cup (125 ml) extra virgin olive oil

500 g fresh tagliatelle

2 small red chillies, finely chopped

2 cloves garlic, finely chopped

1¾ cups (440 ml) tomato passata

2 handfuls basil leaves

150 g grated parmesan

salt flakes and freshly ground black pepper

Preheat oven to 175°C. Brush eggplant with a little of the olive oil. Place on a baking tray and bake for 40 minutes or until soft and cooked. Set aside until cool enough to handle, then scoop flesh from skin and coarsely chop.

Bring a large saucepan of lightly salted water to the boil. Add tagliatelle and cook for 3–4 minutes, or until al dente. Drain. Heat remaining olive oil in a large, wide frying pan over medium heat. Add chilli and garlic and cook for 2–3 minutes or until fragrant. Add eggplant and cook for 1 minute. Pour in tomato passata, add basil and pasta, then toss well. Add parmesan and toss again. Season with salt and pepper and serve immediately. SERVES 4

Carbonara

For a quick pasta carbonara, poach or fry an egg sunny-side up. Stir egg, chopped crispy pancetta or bacon and chopped flat-leaf parsley through hot cooked pasta. Stir through a little pouring cream if desired. Serve sprinkled with freshly grated parmesan.

< Fusilli with braised artichokes, lamb, mint and peas

The slow cooking in this recipe will reward you with a full-flavoured pasta sauce. You can use preserved artichoke hearts if you wish.

300 ml extra virgin olive oil

4 large fresh artichokes, prepared
    (see page 76) and quartered

salt flakes and freshly ground black pepper

8 cloves garlic, 2 finely chopped
    and 6 finely sliced

2 sprigs thyme

2 bay leaves

½ lemon, juiced

450 ml white wine

900 g lamb leg or shoulder, diced

3 tablespoons plain flour

3 sticks celery, finely sliced

1½ brown onions, chopped

6 cups (1.5 litres) chicken stock

500 g dried fusilli or other short pasta

½ bunch mint, leaves picked and torn

1 cup frozen peas, blanched

Heat 200 ml of the olive oil in a wide heavy-based saucepan over medium heat. Add artichokes, salt and pepper and cook for about 5 minutes or until slightly coloured. Stir in 2 cloves chopped garlic, thyme and 1 bay leaf. Add lemon juice, 200 ml of the wine and a splash of water. Simmer for about 15 minutes or until artichokes are cooked and tender, then cool for 15 minutes. Drain and set aside.

Heat remaining olive oil in a large heavy-based saucepan. Dust lamb with flour and brown over medium heat for about 5 minutes. Season and remove lamb. Add a little more oil if necessary and add celery, sliced garlic, onion and remaining bay leaf. Cook, stirring occasionally for about 8 minutes or until onion is golden. Return lamb to pan, add remaining wine and the stock. Simmer over low heat for 1 hour or until tender.

Bring a large saucepan of lightly salted water to the boil. Add fusilli and cook until al dente. Drain. Add pasta to lamb mixture, then stir in mint, peas and artichoke mixture. Check seasoning and serve. SERVES 4

Linguine with tomato, prawns, peas and basil

Prawns and peas are a knockout combination and this is super-quick to put together.

500 g dried linguine

⅔ cup (160 ml) extra virgin olive oil

10 green (raw) prawns, peeled, deveined
    and cut into small pieces

3 small red chillies, finely sliced

3 cloves garlic, finely sliced

2 large ripe tomatoes, coarsely chopped

1 cup basil leaves, torn

2 cups flat-leaf parsley leaves, torn

½ cup (125 ml) white wine

salt flakes and freshly ground black pepper

extra virgin olive oil, for drizzling

½ cup fresh or frozen green peas, blanched
    and coarsely mashed

Bring a large saucepan of lightly salted water to the boil. Add pasta and cook until al dente.

Meanwhile, heat olive oil in a large saucepan over high heat. Add prawns and cook for 30 seconds. Stir in chilli and garlic. Add tomatoes, basil and parsley and stir. Pour in wine, then season with salt and pepper. Drizzle in a little extra olive oil, then remove pan from heat and add peas. Drain pasta, add to prawn mixture and stir to combine. Serve immediately.
SERVES 4

Speedy mushroom pasta

Cook egg noodles in boiling salted water. Meanwhile, quickly cook a couple of handfuls of mushrooms (any variety) in a large frying pan over high heat with lots of butter, a splash of olive oil and a clove or two of garlic. Season generously, add flat-leaf parsley and remove from heat. Fork through a beaten egg immediately and add pasta and grated parmesan before the egg is cooked. Serve immediately.

Linguine with chopped black mussels and fennel

This is a hearty dish with an intense sauce. The caramelised fennel enriches the sauce and the chopped mussels just scream of the sea.

300 ml white wine

1.5 kg black mussels, scrubbed and bearded

500 g dried linguine

⅔ cup (160 ml) extra virgin olive oil

4 spring onions, sliced

3 small red chillies, finely chopped

4 cloves garlic, chopped

6 anchovy fillets, chopped

1 bulb fennel, finely sliced and fonds reserved (optional), to serve

3 sticks celery, finely sliced

1 pinch saffron threads

3 tablespoons tomato paste

4 ripe roma tomatoes, chopped

5 sprigs flat-leaf parsley, chopped

1 lemon, juiced

1 tablespoon butter

Heat half the wine in a large saucepan. Add mussels in batches and steam, covered, until just opened. Discard any unopened mussels. Remove mussels from shells, strain and reserve cooking liquid. Coarsely chop mussel meat.

Bring a large saucepan of lightly salted water to the boil. Add pasta and cook until al dente. Drain. Heat olive oil in a large heavy-based frying pan over medium heat. Add spring onions, chillies, garlic and anchovies and cook, stirring, for 3–5 minutes. Add fennel and celery and cook for a further 5–8 minutes. Lower the heat, add saffron, tomato paste and tomatoes and stir for 5 minutes. Add remaining wine and reserved juice from mussels and simmer for 8 minutes.

Add mussels, parsley and a splash of water (if necessary) to give the sauce a thick consistency. Add drained pasta, lemon juice and butter and stir. Sprinkle with reserved fennel tops (if using) and serve immediately. SERVES 4

> Spaghetti with blue swimmer crab and vongole

Blue swimmer crabs are delicious when in season. The extra virgin olive oil is important in this pasta so invest in something special. My choice would be a fruity, green style.

250 g cooked blue swimmer crabmeat (about 3 large crabs)

1 kg vongole (clams), steamed and shells removed

500 g dried spaghetti

infusion

15 cherry tomatoes, sliced

1 large clove garlic, finely sliced

1½ small red chillies, finely chopped

¼ cup dill, chopped

½ cup mint leaves, chopped

1 cup flat-leaf parsley leaves, chopped

2 spring onions, finely sliced

100 ml extra virgin olive oil

1 lemon, juiced and zested

salt flakes and freshly ground black pepper

Place infusion ingredients in a large bowl. Stir well and set aside for 10 minutes to allow the flavours to develop.

Combine crabmeat, vongole and their juices in a medium saucepan over low heat and cook for about 4 minutes.

Bring a large saucepan of lightly salted water to the boil. Add pasta and cook until al dente. Drain.

Add seafood to infusion mixture and stir well, then stir through pasta and serve immediately. SERVES 4

Alternatives You can use any cooked seafood in this pasta recipe. Cooked, flaked flathead or blue-eye are great alternatives to the crab.

Eggplant parmigiana

My special addition to this basic eggplant parmigiana is the mascarpone and anchovies, which eliminate the need for a white sauce. The anchovies lift the whole dish. Serve this as soon as you have made it, or reheat the next day, when the flavours will be deliciously intense.

2 large eggplants

¾ cup (110 g) plain flour

3 eggs, lightly beaten with
   3 tablespoons water

2 cups fine breadcrumbs

350 ml olive oil, for frying

100 ml extra virgin olive oil

4 cups (1 litre) tomato passata

1 cup (80 g) grated parmesan

200 g mascarpone

4 anchovy fillets, finely chopped

10 slices fontina cheese (see glossary)

4 sprigs oregano, leaves picked

2 sprigs basil, leaves picked

salt flakes and freshly ground black pepper

Peel eggplants to create a striped effect, then cut lengthways into ½ cm-thick slices. Dust eggplant with flour, then dip into egg wash and then breadcrumbs. Heat olive oil in a large heavy-based frying pan over medium heat. Fry eggplant slices for 1–2 minutes on each side or until golden. Drain on kitchen paper.

Preheat oven to 170°C. Place 2 tablespoons of the extra virgin olive oil in a large ovenproof dish and swirl to cover base. Spread about a third of the tomato passata in base of dish. Sprinkle with 3 tablespoons parmesan. Place mascarpone, anchovies and remaining parmesan in a small bowl and stir to combine.

Place one layer of eggplant slices over the base of the dish. Spoon another third of the tomato passata over eggplant, top with a layer of fontina and spoon over a few dollops of mascarpone mixture. Sprinkle with half the oregano and basil. Repeat layers, seasoning each layer. Finish with cheese and herbs. Drizzle with remaining extra virgin olive oil and cover with foil.

Bake for 25 minutes. Remove foil and bake for a further 15 minutes or until golden.

SERVES 6

Eggplant

Eggplant chips are delicious served with drinks. Cut eggplants into chip shapes with the skin on, then dust in flour and eggwash, and roll in a mix of breadcrumbs and sesame seeds. Deep-fry (or shallow-fry in 3 cm of olive oil). Serve hot with lemon mayonnaise. The kids will love them, too. Or try serving with a couple of grilled lamb cutlets for dinner.

Roasted vegetable and gruyère pasties
This recipe is inspired by Stephanie Alexander's silver beet and potato torte. Serve warm with homemade relish.

pastry

3⅓ cups (500 g) plain flour

½ teaspoon table salt

3 tablespoons olive oil

1 cup (250 ml) cold water

filling

3 × 2 cm slices jap pumpkin,
   cut into 1 cm pieces

2 carrots, peeled and cut into 1 cm pieces

2 large potatoes, peeled and
   cut into 1 cm pieces

3 parsnips, peeled and cut
   into 1 cm pieces

½ celeriac, peeled and cut
   into 1 cm pieces

70 ml extra virgin olive oil

salt flakes and freshly ground black pepper

5 golden shallots, peeled and sliced

3 cloves garlic, finely chopped

2 leeks, trimmed and finely sliced

1 teaspoon ground fennel

5 sprigs flat-leaf parsley, chopped

150 g grated gruyère

1 egg, lightly beaten

100 g ricotta

1 extra egg, beaten with
   1 tablespoon olive oil

sesame seeds (optional)

Preheat oven to 165°C. For the pastry, combine flour and salt in a food processor and, with motor running, drizzle in olive oil. Add water and pulse until mixture just comes together. Knead gently on a lightly floured work surface, then wrap in plastic film and place in the fridge for 2 hours.

To make the filling, combine pumpkin, carrot, potato, parsnip and celeriac in a large baking dish. Add 50 ml of the olive oil and season with salt and pepper. Roast vegetables for 1 hour, turning occasionally. Turn off oven and leave vegetables inside for 1 hour (they should shrink and intensify in flavour).

Heat remaining olive oil in a large saucepan over low heat. Add shallots, garlic and leek and cook for 8–10 minutes or until soft and caramelised. Stir in ground fennel and parsley. Add roasted vegetables and stir gently to combine. Stir in gruyère and beaten egg. Adjust seasoning if necessary.

Preheat oven to 200°C. Divide pastry into 4 pieces, making 2 slightly larger than the others. Roll the 2 larger pieces on a lightly floured surface to 5 mm-thick ovals. Spread vegetable mixture evenly on each, leaving a 2 cm border. Scatter ricotta over vegetables. Roll remaining pastry into 2 thin ovals and cover vegetables. Press and twist edges of pastry to seal and glaze tops by brushing with beaten egg. Sprinkle with sesame seeds, if using, and salt and pepper. Place pasties on a large baking tray lined with baking paper. Bake for 25–30 minutes or until cooked and golden. Remove from oven and leave for 10 minutes before serving. Makes 2 large pasties.
SERVES 6–8 AS A LIGHT LUNCH

Whole roasted snapper with rosemary garlic butter and kipfler potatoes

Fish cooked on the bone tends to be far more juicy and flavoursome than seared fillets, and whole fish is easy to prepare. Simply bake it in the oven and serve it straight to the table. I find snapper bones are the easiest to navigate and this recipe features the especially scrumptious combination of snapper, rosemary butter and white wine. I like to cook it with a few kipfler potatoes thrown in to give it a bit of oomph.

4 large sprigs rosemary

200 g unsalted butter, softened

3 cloves garlic, finely sliced

salt flakes and freshly ground black pepper

¼ bunch flat-leaf parsley leaves, very finely chopped

4 snapper or rock flathead, cleaned (350–450 g each)

80–100 ml extra virgin olive oil

1 lemon, thinly sliced

400 ml dry white wine

400 ml fish stock

8 kipfler potatoes, peeled, boiled and halved

2 bunches English spinach, washed and trimmed

120 g mascarpone

Preheat oven to 180°C. Remove leaves from rosemary and chop very finely. Place rosemary, butter, garlic, salt, pepper and parsley in a small bowl and stir to combine. Set aside.

Cut two or three diagonal slits on each side of the fish. Heat the oil in a large non-stick frying pan over high heat. Add fish and fry for about 2–3 minutes on each side, until browned. Season well and transfer to one or two large, lightly greased baking dishes. Spoon knobs of rosemary butter into cavities and on top of fish. Lay lemon slices over fish. Pour wine and stock over and around fish and sit potatoes around fish. Bake for 20–25 minutes or until fish is just cooked (the eyes should be firm and white when cooked).

Remove fish and potatoes from baking dish and keep warm. Place baking dish with reserved juices over medium heat. Stir in spinach and mascarpone and continue stirring for about 2 minutes or until spinach is wilted. Season with salt and pepper.

To serve, transfer whole fish to plates, with potatoes and spinach to the side.
SERVES 4

Pan-fried snapper with fennel, parsley and cherry tomatoes

The flavour of fennel mixed with heaps of parsley and chopped tomato, dressed with oil, lemon and a hint of chilli, gives you a simple, refreshing salad to eat with just about any pan-fried or chargrilled fish. Leaving the salad to sit for a short while lets the flavours develop.

1 large bulb fennel, trimmed and
    fronds reserved

2 small red chillies, very finely sliced

½ clove garlic, finely chopped

1 cup mint leaves, torn

½ bunch flat-leaf parsley leaves,
    finely chopped

salt flakes and freshly ground black pepper

1 lemon, juiced and finely zested

¾ cup (190 ml) extra virgin olive oil

1 punnet (250 g) cherry tomatoes, quartered

4 × 120 g snapper fillets, skin on

extra olive oil

lemon wedges, to serve

To make the salad, thinly slice fennel lengthways and place in a bowl with reserved fennel tops. Add chilli, garlic, mint and parsley and season with salt and pepper. Stir in lemon juice, zest and olive oil. Add tomatoes, then use the back of a wooden spoon to squash slightly to release juices. Leave for 15 minutes to allow the flavours to develop.

Use a little extra olive oil to brush the fish lightly on both sides, then season to taste. Heat a non-stick frying pan over medium heat until hot. Place fish in pan, skin-side down, and cook for 2–3 minutes or until skin is crisp. Turn and cook for 30 seconds on the other side.

To serve, arrange fish on plates, top with fennel salad and add lemon wedges. SERVES 4

> Escalopes of ocean trout with peas, asparagus, lemon cream and pancetta

Instead of ocean trout, you can use kingfish, salmon, garfish or whatever fish is good on the day. Get your fishmonger to cut the fish into slices on a large angle so you get nice escalopes (that is, flattened fillets) with the skin on.

1 cup frozen peas

1 bunch asparagus, sliced diagonally

12 basil leaves, torn

freshly ground black pepper

3 tablespoons extra virgin olive oil

4 × 220 g ocean trout escalopes, skin on

½ cup (125 ml) pouring cream

1 lemon, finely zested

50 g butter

6 slices pancetta (see glossary), grilled until crisp, crumbled

lemon wedges, to serve

Blanch peas for 2 minutes in a small saucepan of lightly salted boiling water. Remove and drain. Crush peas with the back of a spoon. Blanch asparagus in the same water. Remove and drain. Place peas and asparagus in a medium-sized bowl, add basil leaves, pepper and half the olive oil and stir gently to combine.

Heat a non-stick frying pan over medium heat until very hot. Brush remaining oil over the fish, and sear on each side for 1–2 minutes for medium rare, or a little longer if preferred.

Place cream and lemon zest in a small saucepan over medium heat and when simmering, add butter and stir to melt. Pour lemon cream over pea mixture and toss gently. Place trout on 4 plates. Spoon peas and asparagus over fish and top with crumbled pancetta. Serve with lemon wedges.
SERVES 4

Livornese seafood stew

Livornese seafood stew I like to call this the Ferrari of stews. You can use any super-fresh seafood you like. Invite lots of friends and family around and serve straight from the pot.

2 desiree potatoes, peeled and
    cut into 3 cm pieces

6 cups (1.5 litres) fish stock

800 g mussels, scrubbed and
    debearded

500 g vongole (clams)

400 ml white wine

100 ml extra virgin olive oil

1 carrot, peeled and finely sliced

3 sticks celery, finely sliced

4 golden shallots, finely sliced

2 pinches saffron threads

6 cloves garlic, finely sliced

½ bunch oregano leaves

salt flakes, to taste

2 tablespoons tomato paste

2 raw blue swimmer crabs,
    cleaned, cut into quarters

1 × 400 g can tomatoes, crushed

1 cup cooked small pasta
    (such as stelline or risoni)

400 g flathead fillets, cut into
    3 cm pieces

200 g cleaned calamari, cut into
    5 mm rings, or baby octopus

8 large green (raw) prawns, peeled
    and deveined

½ bunch basil leaves

crusty bread, to serve

Place potatoes in a small saucepan and add enough stock to just cover potatoes. Bring to the boil, then simmer over medium heat for 10–15 minutes or until potatoes are tender. Drain.

Place mussels and vongole in a medium saucepan. Add half the wine and steam over high heat, covered, just until shells open. Transfer mussels and vongole to a bowl and set aside. Strain and reserve cooking liquid.

Heat half the oil in a very large saucepan over medium heat. Add carrot, celery, shallots, saffron, garlic and oregano and stir for 8 minutes or until vegetables are caramelised. Stir in salt, tomato paste and crabs, then add tomatoes, potatoes and cooked pasta.

Add the mussels, vongole, fish, calamari or octopus, prawns and 1 cup of reserved cooking liquid to the pan. Add remaining wine and bring to a simmer. Add enough fish stock to cover. Finally, add basil leaves and remaining olive oil and simmer gently for 5 minutes. Serve with cooking juices ladled over and plenty of crusty bread. SERVES 4

Storing seafood Seafood is best cooked the day you buy it. But if you do have to store fish or shellfish overnight, drain the juices, then cover with a damp tea towel or wet paper towel and refrigerate.

Make friends with your fishmonger – it's the best way to learn about seafood.

Seafood pie with rough puff pastry

This seafood pie has a Greek influence and is a lighter alternative to the traditional meat pie. Serve it straight from the oven to table with a green salad.

rough puff pastry

3⅓ cups (500 g) plain flour

1 teaspoon table salt

400 g chilled unsalted butter,
  cut into 2 cm cubes

squeeze of lemon juice

225 ml cold water

filling

60 g butter

2 pinches saffron threads

3 tablespoons plain flour

800 ml fish stock

2 desiree potatoes, peeled
  and sliced

1 bunch spring onions, cut into
  4 cm lengths and blanched

½ cup fresh or frozen peas

½ cup (125 ml) olive oil

12 golden shallots, peeled and sliced

5 cloves garlic, finely sliced

3 leeks, trimmed and sliced

1 tablespoon ras el hanout
  (see glossary)

2 teaspoons ground fennel

salt flakes and freshly ground black pepper

300 g flathead fillets, cut into small pieces

150 g green (raw) prawns, peeled and
  deveined

150 g scallops

1 lemon, juiced and zested

2 sprigs dill, chopped

½ cup medium Iranian couscous
  (see glossary)

1 egg, lightly beaten

To make pastry, sift flour and salt onto a work surface. Rub butter into flour. Add lemon juice and water and mix to a soft dough. Roll out pastry and shape into a rectangle, then roll flat and fold into thirds. Turn the dough so the open end is facing you, then roll out to a rectangle (you may need to lightly flour the surface). Repeat this process. Wrap in plastic film and place in the fridge for 30 minutes. Repeat this process twice, leaving pastry to rest each time.

To make the filling, place 50 g of the butter in a large heavy-based saucepan over medium heat. When butter has melted, add saffron and flour and cook, stirring, for 1 minute. Whisk in stock, increase heat and bring to the boil, then simmer for 3 minutes. Add potato and cook for 5 minutes. Remove from heat, add spring onions and peas, then set aside.

In another saucepan, heat half the olive oil and the remaining butter over medium heat. Stir in shallots, garlic, leek, ras el hanout and fennel. Season and cook, stirring constantly, for 12 minutes, then set aside.

Add remaining oil to a large frying pan over medium heat. When hot, add fish and sear for 1 minute. Remove fish from pan, then sear prawns and then scallops. Remove from heat. Return all seafood to pan, add lemon juice and zest and dill. Boil couscous for 5 minutes, drain and add to pan. Season, then stir seafood mixture into potato mixture. Add shallot mixture and stir. Transfer to a large ovenproof dish.

Preheat oven to 220°C. Roll pastry on a lightly floured surface until 1 cm thick and at least 3 cm larger than dish. Score pastry, decorate top if desired and glaze with beaten egg. Lift pastry onto top of dish. Do not press onto rim – you want the pastry to shrink and 'float' on top of filling. Bake for 20–25 minutes or until pastry is golden and cooked. SERVES 6–8

Storing pastry

The rough puff pastry can be wrapped in plastic film and frozen for up to three months.

Fried mustard and rosemary chicken on rocket with corn salad

This recipe is a family and restaurant favourite – something to do with biting through crispy crunchy skin and discovering the sweet mustard- and garlic-infused flesh underneath, I think. To achieve this perfectly, marinate the chicken overnight, but you could get away with just 2 hours.

4 cloves garlic

4 tablespoons salt flakes

4 sprigs rosemary, leaves picked

1 lemon, juiced and zested

2 tablespoons freshly ground black pepper

½ cup (140 g) Dijon mustard

1 x 1.6 kg free-range chicken, chopped into 8 pieces

2 cups (300 g) plain flour, seasoned with salt and pepper

canola oil, for deep frying

2 corn cobs

½ red onion, halved and sliced

4 sprigs flat-leaf parsley, leaves picked

splash of red-wine vinegar

4 handfuls rocket leaves

Place garlic, salt and rosemary in a mortar and pestle and pound until you have a green, moist salt. Add lemon juice and zest, pepper and mustard, combine and transfer to a plastic bag. Add chicken pieces and toss to coat thoroughly. Set aside to marinate for 2–24 hours in the fridge.

Preheat oven to 200°C.

Toss chicken pieces in seasoned flour. Deep fry for 5 minutes, or until golden, in oil heated to 180°C in a deep fryer or heavy based saucepan. Drain chicken pieces on paper towel and transfer to a baking dish. Bake for 7 minutes, then remove from oven and allow to rest for 2 minutes.

Meanwhile, bring a large saucepan of water to the boil. Reduce heat, add corn cobs and simmer for 5–10 minutes until cooked. Cut kernels from cobs and combine with onion, parsley and vinegar. Place a handful of rocket leaves on each plate and arrange chicken pieces on top. Scatter over corn salad and serve. SERVES 4

> Roast spiced chicken on harissa with herbs and watercress

If you have time, marinate the chicken for at least an hour so that the spice flavours can really sink into the meat.

3 teaspoon baharat (see glossary)

2 teaspoons ground fennel

5 large cloves garlic, crushed

2½ teaspoons salt flakes

freshly ground black pepper

3 sprigs thyme

1 x 1.4 kg free-range chicken, butterflied with breast bone attached

¾ cup (180 ml) extra virgin olive oil

½ cup (125 ml) fresh harissa (see page 194)

flat-leaf parsley and coriander or mint leaves, and watercress sprigs, to serve

lime wedges (optional), to serve

For the marinade, place baharat, fennel, garlic, salt, 10 grinds black pepper and thyme in a small bowl and stir well to combine. Make horizontal cuts through flesh of chicken breast and legs. Rub marinade well into skin. Place chicken in a plastic bag and leave in fridge for at least 1 hour.

Preheat oven to 220°C. Heat olive oil in a large frying pan over high heat. Place chicken in pan and brown on all sides. Transfer to a baking dish and roast for 40–50 minutes or until cooked through and golden.

To serve, spread harissa on a platter, place chicken on top, scatter with sprigs of herbs and watercress and add lime wedges, if using. SERVES 4

Free-range chicken with lemon, thyme, garlic and smashed potatoes

You can't go past roast chicken and potatoes – for me it is the perfect comfort food at any time of the year. I like to serve a roast dinner with a leaf salad – perfect for mopping up the juices.

8 medium desiree potatoes

1 × 1.3 to 1.6 kg free-range chicken

60 g butter, chopped

8 sprigs thyme, crushed

salt flakes and freshly ground
    black pepper

200 ml extra virgin olive oil

1 lemon, halved

3 bulbs garlic, unpeeled and
    separated into cloves

1 brown onion, sliced into thick rings

½ cup (125 ml) water

green salad, to serve

Place unpeeled potatoes in a large saucepan of lightly salted water over medium heat. Bring to the boil, then cook for 25 minutes or until tender. Drain.

Preheat oven to 240°C. Gently separate skin from chicken breasts. Slide knobs of butter and half the thyme under the skin. Rub chicken with salt and pepper. Pour half the oil over the chicken. Squeeze half a lemon over chicken, then place squeezed lemon inside cavity. Use the back of a large knife to lightly crush about a quarter of the garlic, then place crushed garlic in cavity. Scatter onion rings over the base of a baking dish and place the chicken on top. Slice remaining lemon half. Scatter lemon and remaining garlic around chicken. Sprinkle remaining thyme over chicken and into cavity.

Gently press potatoes with a potato masher until skins burst and they are about 2 cm thick. Place around chicken in baking dish, drizzle with remaining olive oil and sprinkle with salt. Pour water into baking pan. Roast chicken for 1 hour or until the juices run clear when flesh is pierced with a skewer. Remove from oven and set aside to rest for 5–10 minutes before serving.

Carve the chicken, drizzle with the pan juices and serve with roast potatoes and garlic and a dressed green salad. SERVES 4

Tuscan chicken This marinade is also great with lamb leg chops. Serve with a simple potato salad (or baked potatoes) and a dressed salad of rocket and radicchio.

4 cloves garlic, coarsely chopped

2 sprigs rosemary, leaves picked and
    coarsely chopped

4 tablespoons Dijon mustard

⅓ cup (80 ml) extra virgin olive oil

2 lemons, juiced and zested

salt flakes and freshly ground black pepper

1 × 1.5 kg chicken, cut into 8 pieces

lemon wedges, to serve

To make the marinade, place garlic and rosemary in a small bowl. Add mustard, olive oil, lemon juice and zest. Stir well to combine and season to taste. Pour marinade over chicken, cover and leave in fridge for 40 minutes or overnight.

Preheat a barbecue to hot, then cook chicken, skin-side down, for 8–10 minutes. Turn chicken, reduce heat and cook for a further 8–10 minutes or until cooked through. Transfer to a platter, keep warm and allow to rest for 2 minutes before serving with lemon wedges. SERVES 6

> **Roast chicken with green olives, almonds and oregano** Just smash everything up, dunk the chicken in the marinade and cook it in one dish. Too simple.

1 cup (160 g) blanched almonds, coarsely chopped

80 g pitted green olives, chopped

1 cup flat-leaf parsley leaves, finely chopped

1 bunch oregano leaves, finely chopped

2 green chillies, sliced

100 ml extra virgin olive oil

freshly ground black pepper

2 small red chillies, finely chopped

4 cloves garlic, finely chopped

1 lemon, juiced and zested

salt flakes

1½ tablespoons Dijon mustard

4 free-range chicken marylands, jointed

3 large desiree potatoes, peeled and finely sliced

2 red onions, sliced into rings

½ cup (125 ml) water

½ cup (125 ml) white wine

Preheat oven to 200°C. Place almonds, olives, parsley, oregano and green chillies in a large bowl, drizzle with a little of the olive oil and stir to combine. Season with pepper.

Combine red chilli, garlic, lemon juice and zest, salt, pepper and mustard and coat chicken pieces. Set aside for 10 minutes.

Heat remaining oil in a heavy-based frying pan over high heat. Add chicken, brown on all sides and remove from heat. Add chicken to the prepared almond marinade.

Lightly grease an ovenproof dish and add potato and onion. Top with chicken pieces and pour over any remaining marinade, along with water and wine. Cover with foil and bake for 15 minutes. Remove foil and bake for a further 10–15 minutes or until chicken is golden and cooked. Serve immediately. SERVES 4

Herbed almond crumbs Crush raw almonds and combine with fresh breadcrumbs, parsley and lemon zest. Use this mix to crumb fresh fish before pan-frying and serving with a watercress salad – perfect for the warmer months.

Vintners' chicken with tarragon

This is my version of a dish traditionally made by vintners (wine merchants), who use the leftover grapes, juice and must after picking.

1 × size 12 to 14 free-range chicken,
    cut into 8 pieces

salt flakes and freshly ground black pepper

8 large kipfler potatoes, scrubbed
    and boiled for 10 minutes,
    then cut lengthways

2 small bulbs garlic, cloves
    separated and bruised

½ cup (125 ml) extra virgin olive oil

4 sprigs thyme

10 sprigs French tarragon

500 g muscatel grapes, cut into small
    bunches and slightly crushed

Preheat oven to 160°C. Season chicken with salt and pepper. Fry chicken in a lightly greased heavy-based frying pan over medium heat for 5–6 minutes or until golden brown (you may need to do this in batches). Place potatoes, garlic, olive oil, thyme and half the tarragon in a medium-sized bowl and stir to combine. Season. Lay potato mixture over the base of a large baking dish, then top with chicken pieces. Scatter over remaining sprigs of tarragon and half the grapes.

Cover with foil and bake for 15 minutes. Uncover, scatter remaining grapes over chicken, then increase heat to 180°C and bake for a further 15–20 minutes or until chicken is golden, crispy and cooked through. SERVES 4

> Celeriac remoulade with grilled chicken

I love this remoulade with chicken but it is also great with grilled or roasted mid-loin pork chops, steak or even with smoked trout in a salad.

2 tablespoons Dijon mustard

1 tablespoon wholegrain mustard

150 g mayonnaise (whole-egg
    and, if possible, homemade)

3 tablespoons cream, lightly whipped

¼ lemon, juiced

½ red onion, finely chopped

1 large celeriac, peeled and cut
    into fine matchsticks

1 nashi pear, cut into fine matchsticks

salt flakes and freshly ground black pepper

2 chicken breast fillets

⅔ cup (100 g) toasted hazelnuts,
    coarsely chopped, to serve

watercress, to serve

lemon wedges, to serve

To make the remoulade, place mustards, mayonnaise, cream and lemon juice in a medium bowl and whisk until smooth. Add onion, celeriac and pear and gently combine. Season and set aside for 15 minutes.

Slice chicken breasts in half horizontally, place between 2 sheets of baking paper, and use a mallet to flatten. Preheat a chargrill plate until hot and cook chicken fillets for about 1½ minutes on each side or until cooked through. Top chicken with remoulade, scatter with hazelnuts and watercress and serve with lemon wedges. SERVES 4

Free-range chicken with bruschetta, porcini, chicken liver and rosemary stuffing

Ask your butcher to bone the chicken, leaving the drumsticks and wings intact and all the skin on. This technique means the flavours permeate the chicken more intensely and it cooks so much faster.

10 g dried porcini mushrooms, soaked in 1 cup (250 ml) boiling water for 3 minutes

150 ml extra virgin olive oil

1 brown onion, chopped

3 cloves garlic, chopped

3 sprigs rosemary, leaves picked and finely chopped

3 sprigs thyme, leaves picked

6 thick slices bread, toasted and rubbed lightly with garlic and drizzled with olive oil

200 g chicken livers, trimmed of fat and soaked in milk for 30 minutes

150 g unsalted butter, chopped

salt flakes and freshly ground black pepper

1 cup flat-leaf parsley leaves, coarsely chopped

60 ml sherry or red-wine vinegar

1 × 1.4 kg free-range chicken, boned but with wings and drumsticks intact

1 bunch rosemary (optional)

For the stuffing, drain porcini mushrooms, reserving liquid, and coarsely chop. Heat a little of the olive oil in a frying pan over medium heat. Cook the onion and garlic for 3 minutes or until onion is soft. Add mushrooms, rosemary and thyme, then transfer to a bowl.

Break bruschetta into small pieces and add to onion mixture with reserved porcini liquid. Drain livers well. Heat a little olive oil in a frying pan over medium heat. Add livers and brown on both sides for 1½ minutes, then stir in a knob of butter. Place livers on a plate and season. When cool, coarsely chop. Combine livers, parsley and half the remaining butter with bruschetta mixture. Use your hands to mix well, season, add sherry or vinegar, then press together.

Preheat oven to 230°C. Place chicken on work surface, skin-side down, and season. Form stuffing into an oval and press into the cavity of the chicken. Pull skin to seal cavity and secure with metal skewers. Gently separate skin from chicken breasts. Slide remaining butter under the skin. Brush chicken with a little olive oil and season.

Heat a little olive oil in a large frying pan, add chicken, breast-side down, and brown for 3 minutes. Transfer to a lightly greased baking dish and place on top of rosemary, if using. Roast chicken for 50–60 minutes or until golden and cooked through (juices will run clear when flesh is pierced with a skewer). Set aside to rest for 10 minutes before carving. SERVES 4

Chicken For a healthy, fun takeaway lunch on the beach, buy a roasted free-range chicken with stuffing, along with an iceberg lettuce and salt. Tear off a lettuce leaf, place some chicken and stuffing in it, sprinkle with salt, then roll it up to eat. For a change from chicken, try it with prawns and mayonnaise.

Cardamom, oregano and verjuice marinated quail

This unusual but delicious combination works best paired with a fresh salad. Try a combination of orange, red onion and parsley, or a tabbouleh – but replace the tomato with sliced green or black seedless grapes. If preferred, use chicken instead of quail.

10 cardamom pods, seeds removed from husk

1 tablespoon freshly ground black pepper

1 lemon, zested

2 teaspoons salt flakes

3 cloves garlic

⅓ cup (80 ml) extra virgin olive oil

1½ tablespoons Dijon mustard

2 tablespoons dried oregano

6 quails, butterflied, or 6 chicken thigh fillets

1 cup (250 ml) verjuice

lemon wedges, to serve

To make the marinade, combine cardamom seeds, pepper, lemon zest and salt in a mortar and pestle and grind to a powder. Add garlic and half the olive oil and pound to form a paste. Stir in mustard, oregano and remaining oil.

Place quails or chicken in a large dish, rub in marinade and pour over verjuice. Cover dish and place in the fridge for at least 4 hours.

Drain marinade from quails or chicken, then season with extra salt, if desired. Preheat barbecue or oiled frying pan over medium heat and cook quails for 8–10 minutes (cook chicken for 10–15 minutes) or until cooked through and browned on both sides. Serve with lemon wedges. SERVES 6 AS A STARTER

> Twice-cooked duck with radicchio salad

Duck has a rich, intense flavour so I like to serve it with sharp or acidic flavours such as balsamic vinegar or vincotto.

2 × size 24 ducks (thigh bones released and wishbones and neck removed and excess fat removed – ask your butcher to do this)

3 tablespoons salt flakes

1 tablespoon freshly ground black pepper

1 teaspoon Chinese five-spice powder

1 tablespoon olive oil

2 heads radicchio, trimmed

1 red onion, halved and finely sliced

150 ml vincotto (see glossary) or aged balsamic vinegar

100 ml extra virgin olive oil

salt flakes and freshly ground black pepper

½ bunch watercress sprigs (optional)

spaetzle (dumplings), mashed potato or cooked buttered noodles with parmesan, to serve

Place ducks on a tray, uncovered, in the fridge for 12 hours before cooking.

Preheat oven to 225°C. Combine salt, pepper, Chinese five-spice and olive oil in a mortar and pestle and grind until smooth. Rub the salt mixture into the ducks, inside and out. Prick the ducks all over with a fork and place on a roasting rack in a baking dish. Roast on middle shelf of oven for 1 hour. Remove from oven and set aside to rest for 20 minutes.

Turn up oven to 230°C. Cut ducks down both sides of the backbone, then turn over and cut diagonally down both sides of the breastbone to the thigh. Use a knife to remove the skin and meat from each half, keeping each half in one piece (the leg will still be on the bone). Transfer duck halves to two baking trays lined with baking paper. Roast for 15 minutes or until skin is crisp.

Meanwhile, shred radicchio finely and place in a bowl. Add onion, vincotto and olive oil and season. If using watercress, add it now, and toss gently to combine. Serve duck with radicchio salad and spaetzle, mash or noodles. SERVES 4

Twice-cooked duck with braised witlof and mandarin

When mandarins are in season they are a terrific alternative to orange, which is duck's traditional match. Leaving the ducks uncovered in the fridge for 12 hours before cooking helps the skin become crispy when roasted.

2 × size 24 ducks (thigh bones released and wishbones and neck removed and excess fat removed – ask your butcher to do this)

3 tablespoons salt flakes

1 tablespoon freshly ground black pepper

1 teaspoon Chinese five-spice powder

1 tablespoon olive oil

60 g butter

4 witlof, cut in half

100 g ginger, grated

salt flakes and freshly ground black pepper

3 mandarins, zested and juiced

450 ml chicken stock

3 mandarins, extra

½ bunch spring onions, finely sliced

2 knobs butter, extra

Place ducks on a tray, uncovered, in the fridge for 12 hours before cooking.

Preheat oven to 225°C. Combine salt, pepper, Chinese five-spice and olive oil in a mortar and pestle and grind until smooth. Rub ducks inside and out with the salt mixture. Prick the ducks all over with a fork and place on a roasting rack in a baking dish. Roast on middle shelf of oven for 1 hour. Remove from oven and set aside to rest for 20 minutes.

Turn up oven to 230°C. Cut ducks down both sides of the backbone, then turn over and cut down both sides of the breastbone to the thigh. Use a knife to remove the skin and meat from each half, keeping each half in one piece (the leg will still be on the bone). Transfer duck halves to 2 baking trays lined with baking paper. Roast for 15 minutes or until skin is crisp.

Melt the butter in a large heavy-based saucepan over medium heat. Add witlof, ginger, salt and pepper and cook until witlof is golden brown. Stir in mandarin zest and juice and bring to the boil. Simmer for 2 minutes. Add stock and simmer for 8 minutes or until witlof is tender and sauce is reduced. Cut extra mandarins into three sections crossways, then peel. Add mandarins, spring onions and extra butter to sauce and stir. Spoon sauce over roasted duck and serve. SERVES 4

Duck If you have leftover cooked duck meat, cut it into small slices. Heat a little olive oil in a frying pan and fry duck until crispy. Season and add to a bowl of sliced boiled potato, watercress, orange segments and witlof leaves. Sprinkle with hazelnuts and a dash of sherry vinegar.

Mid-loin pork chops with orange, fennel and rosemary

If you have time, leave the chops in the orange zest, fennel and rosemary mixture for at least 30 minutes for the flavours to blend.

2 tablespoons fennel seeds

1 tablespoon black peppercorns

2 tablespoons orange zest

3 sprigs rosemary, leaves picked and finely chopped

4 organic rindless pork loin chops

salt flakes and freshly ground black pepper

3 tablespoons olive oil

2 oranges, juiced

600 ml beef stock

100 g butter, chopped

mashed potato, to serve

Preheat oven to 180°C. Combine fennel seeds, peppercorns, orange zest and rosemary leaves in a mortar and pestle and grind into a fine powder. Press fennel mixture onto chops and set aside to rest for 30 minutes.

Season chops with salt. Heat olive oil in a heavy-based ovenproof frying pan over high heat. Add chops and brown for 4 minutes on each side. Add orange juice and stock. Cover with foil and bake for 10 minutes. Transfer chops to another dish and keep warm. Boil juices in pan over high heat for 2 minutes or until sauce is reduced. Check seasoning, add butter and stir to combine. Serve chops with sauce spooned over. Serve with creamy mashed potato. SERVES 4

Fennel Finely shaved fennel adds a crisp, fresh bite to any salad. Bring out its unique flavour by dressing with a little extra virgin olive oil, salt flakes and a squeeze of lemon juice.

Rolled pork belly with apple and red onion

This is my interpretation of *porchetta di maiale*, which can be served hot, warm or cold. It gives me flashbacks of wonderful childhood meals and is typical of the style of dish I share with my family at Christmas. The yellow pepper salad I serve with the pork should be sharp and sweet at the same time, to complement the richness of the pork.

1 × 2.5 kg boneless pork belly

4 litres boiling water

3 large bulbs garlic, roasted for 30 minutes at 150°C, flesh removed and mashed

5 tablespoons freshly ground fennel seeds

12 very thin slices pancetta (see glossary)

20 sage leaves

salt flakes and freshly ground black pepper

6 red onions

6 bay leaves

2 tablespoons olive oil

8 small apples, scored in a ring

500 ml water

100 ml white wine

250 ml chicken stock

jap pumpkin wedges, roasted with olive oil, cinnamon and salt, to serve

sweet yellow pepper salad

15 banana capsicums (see glossary)

100 ml extra virgin olive oil

30 ml white–wine vinegar

salt flakes and freshly ground black pepper

2 pinches castor sugar

½ bunch flat-leaf parsley, chopped

Preheat oven to 240°C. Place pork on a rack, skin-side up, and pour 4 litres of boiling water over skin to soften. Transfer the pork to a chopping board and use a very sharp knife to score the skin. Rub flesh with mashed roasted garlic and half the fennel seeds. Drape pancetta over flesh, scatter over sage leaves and season with salt and pepper. Roll pork and tie securely with kitchen string at 3–4 cm intervals. Mix remaining ground fennel with salt and pepper and rub into scored skin.

Peel onions and cut in half. Spread onions over a lightly greased large baking dish, add bay leaves and place pork on top. Pour oil over pork and roast for 25 minutes or until skin starts to crackle. Place apples around pork and add 500 ml water to the pan. Lower the temperature to 150°C and roast for 1–1½ hours or until skin is golden and pork is cooked through.

Remove pork and allow to rest, covered loosely with foil, for 15 minutes. Transfer apples and onions to another dish and keep warm. Skim fat from pan juices, add wine and stir over high heat to deglaze pan. Add stock and boil over high heat until thickened and reduced by one-third. Check seasoning. Strain.

Serve sliced pork on a platter with apples and onions. Pour sauce over. Serve with roasted jap pumpkin wedges and sweet yellow pepper salad.

To make the salad, roast banana capsicums at 200°C for 12 minutes. Cool, peel, deseed and cut into 2 cm dice. Dress with extra virgin olive oil and white-wine vinegar and season with salt, pepper and sugar. SERVES 8

Porchetta This porchetta is perfect for leftovers. Thinly slice the cold meat and make a delicious sandwich with fresh apple, pepper and lots of rocket.

Rabbit braised with green grapes and almonds

The ground almonds thicken the cooking juices and the grapes add a delicious sweetness, making this braise less robust and much lighter. It makes a beautiful autumn or end-of-summer meal.

1 × 1.5 kg rabbit, cut into 8 pieces

3 tablespoons extra virgin olive oil

salt flakes and freshly ground black pepper

3 slices pancetta (see glossary)

2 large brown onions, coarsely chopped

1 celery heart, coarsely chopped

8 cloves garlic, chopped

1 bay leaf

50 g butter

½ cup (60 g) ground almonds

3 desiree potatoes, peeled and cut
   into chunks

400 g seedless green grapes

½ cup (125 ml) white wine

2 cups (500 ml) chicken stock

80 g muscatel grapes

lettuce and cress salad, to serve

Rub the rabbit pieces with some of the olive oil, then season with salt and pepper. Place remaining olive oil in a large, heavy-based saucepan over high heat. When the oil is hot, add rabbit and cook for 5 minutes or until brown. Add pancetta and stir.

Remove rabbit from pan. Reduce heat to low. Add onion, celery, garlic and bay leaf and cook, stirring, for 6 minutes or until onion is soft. Add butter and ground almonds and stir until ground almonds are lightly browned. Stir in the potato, rabbit, seedless grapes and wine. Pour in stock, cover and simmer for 30 minutes. Add muscatel grapes, adjust seasoning if necessary and simmer for 10 minutes or until rabbit is tender.

Serve with a lettuce and cress salad with heaps of freshly snipped herbs such as flat-leaf parsley, tarragon and chervil. SERVES 4

> Rabbit braised with pancetta, sage, verjuice and spring onions

Fresh rabbit is readily available these days from good butchers and poultry suppliers and adds a hearty flavour to this dish. If you like, you can substitute chicken for the rabbit.

1 × 1.5 kg rabbit, cut into 6 pieces
   (or 1.5 kg chicken, cut into 6 pieces)

salt flakes and freshly ground black pepper

50 ml olive oil

50 g butter

100 g pancetta (see glossary), sliced

8 golden shallots, halved

1 bay leaf

6 sprigs sage

2 sprigs thyme

2 sticks celery, finely sliced

8 cloves garlic, chopped

350 ml verjuice or white wine

2 parsnips, peeled and sliced

6 prunes, pitted

4 cups (1 litre) chicken stock

mashed potato or cooked small pasta
   (such as risoni), to serve

Preheat oven to 180°C. Season rabbit with salt and pepper. Heat oil and half the butter in a large, heavy-based, ovenproof casserole dish over high heat. Add the rabbit pieces and brown on all sides. Stir in pancetta, spring onions, bay leaf and herbs. Add celery and garlic and cook over low heat for 6 minutes or until onions are golden and soft. Add verjuice or wine and bring to a simmer. Add parsnips and prunes, pour in stock and simmer for 5 minutes. Reduce heat to low, cover, and cook for 30 minutes.

Remove lid and bake for a further 20 minutes or until rabbit is golden. Stir in remaining butter and serve with mashed potato or pasta. SERVES 4

Spiced lamb on rosemary skewers with puréed spinach and green chilli salad

This dish is inspired by the Turkish 'kofta'-style mince skewers. Using rosemary stems as skewers imparts a gentle herby flavour. The spiced meat works particularly well with the sweet–sour pine nut, currant and mint salad.

500 g minced lamb

1 teaspoon salt flakes

1 teaspoon ground cumin

freshly ground black pepper

1 teaspoon ground cinnamon

8 × 15 cm rosemary stems,
   leaves removed except for 2 cm at end

2 tablespoons olive oil

1 small brown onion, finely chopped

3 cloves garlic, finely chopped

½ small red chilli (or to taste), finely chopped

½ bunch flat-leaf parsley

½ bunch English spinach leaves

½ cup (125 ml) pouring cream

2 tablespoons butter

3 tablespoons pine nuts, to serve

green chilli salad

1 green chilli, seeded and sliced

75 g currants, covered in red-wine vinegar
   and brought to the boil, then drained

½ red onion, finely sliced

½ cup mint leaves, coarsely chopped

Place lamb mince, salt, cumin, pepper and cinnamon in a food processor and process until smooth. Divide lamb mixture evenly into 10 portions and, using lightly oiled hands, mould the meat gently around rosemary skewers. Cover and refrigerate.

Heat 1 tablespoon olive oil in a frying pan over medium heat. Add onion, garlic and red chilli and cook for 5 minutes or until onion is transparent. Stir in parsley and spinach. Pour in cream and cook for 5 minutes. Place spinach mixture and butter in a food processor and process until smooth.

Heat a barbecue or cast-iron chargrill pan and cook skewers, turning occasionally, for 5–8 minutes.

Place green chilli, currants, red onion and mint with remaining oil in a small bowl and toss gently to combine.

To serve, spoon spinach purée onto plates, top with lamb skewers, then sprinkle over green chilli salad and pine nuts. SERVES 4

Lamb shanks braised with cinnamon, garlic and thyme

This dish has strong Middle Eastern overtones, with the heady scent of cinnamon and cumin and slight heat from the chilli. I suggest serving it with a fresh, leafy salad. It's the perfect do-ahead dish for a small dinner party.

4 lamb shanks, knuckles removed

salt flakes and freshly ground black pepper

⅓ cup (80 ml) olive oil

4 sticks celery, finely sliced

80 g pancetta (see glossary), sliced

4 golden shallots, peeled and cut in half

10 cloves garlic, cut into quarters

6 sprigs thyme

1 teaspoon cumin seeds

2 cinnamon sticks

2 small red chillies, split

2 large green chillies, split

1 medium sweet potato, peeled
   and cut into 3 cm pieces

3 desiree potatoes, peeled
   and cut into 3 cm pieces

2 parsnips, peeled and sliced

2 carrots, peeled and sliced

2 tablespoons tomato paste

4 cups (1 litre) chicken stock

Preheat oven to 160°C. Season shanks with salt and pepper. Heat oil in a large, heavy-based ovenproof casserole dish over high heat. Add the shanks and cook for a few minutes, until browned. Remove shanks from dish. Add celery, pancetta, golden shallots, garlic, thyme, cumin and cinnamon and stir well. Add chillies, remaining vegetables and tomato paste and stir again.

Return shanks to the dish, pour in stock and simmer for 2 minutes. Check seasoning and adjust if necessary. Cover dish and bake for 2½ hours or until the meat is very tender and falling off the bone. Serve immediately. SERVES 4

Chargrilled lamb cutlets with oregano and hot fetta dressing

Hot fetta dressing sounds irresistible, doesn't it? Well it is. Fetta with lamb is a beautiful combination, but you could also pour the fetta dressing over hot cannellini beans, broad beans or peas as a vegetable dish to accompany barbecued or roasted meat, or as part of a vegetarian meal.

2 × 6-bone racks of lamb, fat untrimmed

6 cloves garlic

3 tablespoons dried oregano leaves

1 bunch oregano, leaves picked

⅓ cup (80 ml) red-wine vinegar

1 lemon, juiced

200 ml extra virgin olive oil

freshly ground black pepper

8 kipfler potatoes, scrubbed

2 teaspoons salt flakes

1 teaspoon Dijon mustard

150 g marinated fetta, crumbled

16 Ligurian olives

1 bunch curly endive, leaves separated

Score flesh and fat of lamb in a crisscross fashion, then slice into cutlets.

To make the dressing, peel and finely chop 5 cloves of the garlic and place in a small bowl. Stir in dried oregano, half the fresh oregano leaves, 30 ml of the vinegar, half the lemon juice, 3 tablespoons of the olive oil and pepper. Mix well, then rub into lamb cutlets. Cover and set aside in the fridge for 1 hour.

Place potatoes in a medium-sized saucepan, cover with water and bring to boil over high heat. Cook for 10–15 minutes or until tender. Drain, then thickly slice lengthways.

To make fetta dressing, peel and finely chop remaining garlic clove. Place in a small bowl with salt, mustard, remaining vinegar and lemon juice. Add remaining olive oil and whisk well. Season with pepper. Heat a chargrill pan on high and cook cutlets for 2–3 minutes on each side, or until cooked to your liking.

Heat dressing in a small saucepan over medium heat – do not boil. Stir in fetta, olives and remaining fresh oregano leaves.

To serve, place sliced potatoes on plates, scatter with curly endive leaves and top with cutlets. Spoon over hot fetta dressing. SERVES 4

Roasted boned leg of lamb with basil, lemon, almond, oregano and garlic

Buying a boned leg of lamb makes for a much-reduced cooking time. For this recipe, ask your butcher to tunnel-bone a 2 kg leg of lamb. And don't skip the resting time before carving – it's vital to let the meat 'relax'.

½ bunch basil, leaves picked

1 bunch oregano, leaves picked

2 bay leaves

8 cloves garlic, peeled

½ cup (125 ml) extra virgin olive oil

finely grated zest and juice of 2 large lemons

salt flakes and freshly ground black pepper

½ cup (60 g) ground almonds

1 × 2 kg leg lamb, tunnel-boned

baked potatoes and seasonal salad, to serve

Combine herbs, bay leaves and garlic in a food processor or a large mortar and pestle. Add half the olive oil, the lemon zest, salt and pepper. Process until well combined. Add ground almonds and process again. Transfer mixture to a medium bowl. Stir in the remaining olive oil and the lemon juice.

Use a sharp knife to score fat on lamb. Rub herb mixture all over lamb. Cover and set aside to marinate at room temperature for at least 1 hour, or toss it in a plastic bag, place it in the fridge and let it marinate overnight.

Preheat oven to 230°C. Place lamb in a baking dish and bake for 25 minutes, then lower oven temperature to 180°C and bake for a further 20–30 minutes. (If you prefer, the lamb could be cooked in a kettle barbecue.) When cooked, leave the meat to rest in a warm place for 20 minutes before carving. Serve with baked potatoes and seasonal salad. SERVES 6

Traditional osso buco with saffron risotto

Everyone has a favourite osso buco recipe. I hope this traditional version becomes yours.

10 pieces osso buco

⅓ cup (50 g) plain flour

salt flakes and freshly ground black pepper

100 ml extra virgin olive oil

3 slices pancetta (see glossary)

5 cloves garlic, finely sliced

10 golden shallots, peeled

2 bay leaves

1 celery heart, chopped

6 baby carrots, scrubbed and finely sliced

2 sprigs thyme

2 sprigs oregano

2 tablespoons tomato paste

200 ml white wine

700 ml chicken stock

pinch nutmeg

10 cherry tomatoes

saffron risotto

1.2 litres chicken stock

2 pinches saffron threads

100 ml extra virgin olive oil

1 clove garlic, chopped

½ brown onion, chopped

2 cups (400 g) arborio rice

1 bay leaf

150 g grated parmesan

80 g butter

salt flakes and freshly ground
   black pepper

Coat osso buco in flour, shake off excess then season with salt and pepper. Heat olive oil in a large saucepan over high heat. Add osso buco and cook for 6 minutes, browning on all sides. Remove osso buco. Add a little more oil to the pan if necessary, then add pancetta, garlic, shallots, bay leaves, celery, carrots, thyme and oregano sprigs. Cook for 8–10 minutes or until golden. Stir in tomato paste and wine, then return osso buco to pan. Simmer, covered, for 4 minutes. Add stock, nutmeg and tomatoes and simmer for 45 minutes or until meat is just falling off the bone.

To make the risotto, heat stock and saffron in a saucepan over high heat until simmering. Heat olive oil in a large saucepan over high heat. Add garlic and onion and stir until well coated with oil. Add rice and bay leaf and stir until rice is coated with oil and slightly toasted. Add 250 ml simmering stock to rice and stir over medium heat for 5 minutes or until stock is absorbed. Add remaining stock, 125 ml at a time, stirring continuously, allowing each addition to be absorbed before adding the next. After about 20 minutes, when rice is al dente (cooked but with just a little 'bite'), stir in parmesan and butter, then season. Serve the osso buco with saffron risotto.
SERVES 4–6

Maltagliata of beef with rocket, radicchio and ricotta

This is a favourite snack for lunch or dinner. 'Maltagliata' means 'badly cut' in Italian. The meat is cut into strips and pan-fried with balsamic vinegar, then dropped hot into a salad of rocket and radicchio.

300 g rocket, torn into bite-sized pieces

1 head radicchio, torn into bite-sized pieces

½ red onion, finely sliced

4 sprigs flat-leaf parsley, torn

150 ml extra virgin olive oil

½ cup (125 ml) balsamic vinegar

salt flakes and freshly ground black pepper

600 g scotch fillet or rump steak,
   sliced into strips

5 tablespoons plain flour, seasoned

150 g ricotta

Combine rocket, radicchio, onion and parsley in a large bowl. Combine 120 ml of the olive oil, 100 ml of the balsamic vinegar, salt and pepper to make a dressing. Pour over salad leaves and toss gently to coat.

Heat remaining oil in a heavy-based non-stick frying pan over medium heat until hot. Dip beef in flour, shake off excess and fry quickly until golden brown. Add remaining balsamic, stirring quickly to deglaze the pan. Pour beef and juices over salad leaves and toss to combine. Crumble the fresh ricotta over the salad and serve immediately. SERVES 4

Roasted beef eye fillet with buttered oysters, marrow, herbs and mashed potato

This is a modern version of the classic carpet-bag steak. The briny flavours of oysters and the richness of bone marrow paired with beef is a combination not to be missed. This is a sexy dinner party dish.

600 g beef eye fillet

salt flakes and freshly ground
    black pepper

olive oil

4 medium desiree potatoes,
    peeled and cut into chunks

½ cup (125 ml) pouring cream

150 g butter at room temperature

100 g bone marrow (available from butchers)

1 golden shallot, peeled and chopped

1 clove garlic, chopped

½ bunch chives, chopped

6 sprigs watercress, chopped

6 sprigs chervil, chopped

6 sprigs flat-leaf parsley, chopped

12 Pacific oysters, shucked

½ lemon, juiced

extra watercress sprigs, to garnish

Preheat oven to 220°C. Season fillet well with salt and pepper. Place a lightly oiled frying pan over high heat. When pan is hot, add fillet and sear for 3 minutes on each side. Remove from heat.

Place potatoes in heavily salted water, bring to the boil, then cook over medium heat for 15–18 minutes or until cooked. Drain and push through a mouli or potato ricer. Heat cream with 80 g of the butter in a small saucepan. When hot, whisk into potatoes until creamy and smooth. Set aside and keep warm.

Roast fillet in the oven for about 15 minutes for medium-rare or until cooked to your liking. Cover with foil and set aside to rest for 5 minutes.

Cut marrow into pieces. Blanch for 20 seconds in a saucepan of lightly salted simmering water. Strain, set aside and keep warm. Place a frying pan over medium heat, add a knob of butter, shallots and garlic and cook for 2–3 minutes until translucent. Remove pan from heat, then stir in marrow, remaining butter and herbs. Season. Add oysters, return to heat for 1–2 minutes, stir and add lemon juice.

To serve, spoon mashed potatoes on plates, layer with sliced fillet and top with oyster mixture. Grind over black pepper and garnish with watercress sprigs. SERVES 4

Fish If you prefer fish for the main course, leave the bone marrow out of the oyster mixture, add extra lemon juice, and spoon over seared ocean trout fillets (pan-fry for 3 minutes on each side for rare). Serve garnished with watercress and crispy fried shallots.

Mr Godby's oxtail braised with red wine, cloves and pearl onions
Mr Godby is a legendary braiser and friend of mine. This recipe results in rich, gelatinous meat and is perfect with mash.

12 pieces oxtail

2 bay leaves

5 sprigs thyme

800 ml red wine

½ cup (75 g) plain flour

100 g butter

100 ml extra virgin olive oil

8 cups (2 litres) beef stock

12 pearl or pickling onions,
  each studded with 1 clove

6 cloves garlic, chopped

6 Dutch (baby) carrots, scrubbed

1 celery heart, chopped

3 sprigs flat-leaf parsley

4 parsnips, peeled, cut into quarters
  (remove core if it's hard and woody)

salt flakes and freshly ground black pepper

mashed potato, to serve

Place oxtail, bay leaves and thyme sprigs in a large bowl. Add wine, cover bowl with plastic film and place in the fridge overnight.

Drain oxtail, reserving marinade, and dust lightly with flour. Strain marinade, reserving herbs. Heat butter and 1 tablespoon of the olive oil in a large heavy-based saucepan over high heat. Add oxtail and cook for about 6 minutes, browning on all sides. Add reserved marinade, 1 litre of the stock and 2 litres of water, cover and simmer over medium heat for 2½ hours. Skim surface occasionally and add extra water so that it doesn't become dry. Remove from heat. Heat 2 tablespoons olive oil in a large heavy-based pan over medium heat. Add onions, garlic, carrots and celery and cook for 9 minutes or until golden. Add reserved herbs, oxtail, parsley and remaining stock. Simmer for 35 minutes or until meat is just falling off the bone.

Heat remaining olive oil in a frying pan over medium heat. Add parsnip quarters, season and stir. Cook for about 6 minutes, until golden, then add to braise. Simmer for 5 minutes and serve with mashed potato. SERVES 4–6

Sides

A meal is vastly improved by good accompaniments and compromised by bad. In fact, I recommend you take as much care with the carrots as you do with the chicken. In this section I suggest some favourite side dishes, salads, dips and Middle-Eastern condiments, and several mayonnaise sauces that are especially good with grilled and pan-seared fish.

Unfortunately many vegetables are avoided – despised even – by many people. Mostly this is due to a bad experience or rather a long sequence of bad food experiences, commonly known as childhood. Don't blame your mother or father – they were quite busy I'm sure – and certainly don't blame the artichoke, Brussels sprout or cabbage.

I love using unusual or unfashionable vegetables, and grains that are often overlooked or misunderstood. I see them as a challenge. With the right recipe, I'm convinced I can convert the most ardent opponent to these ingredients. Sometimes it may involve a raw artichoke camouflaged in a salad, or coleslaw spiked with radish and parmesan, but always it will rely on the integrity of the ingredients and a little care.

Though of course we can now buy asparagus in July, these recipes are better with local seasonal produce for two reasons: it tastes better and it's less expensive. When a vegetable or fruit is abundant I use it often; when it is not, I look forward to the season when it will be.

Brussels sprouts sautéed with garlic, chervil and cream

I have no fond memories of Brussels sprouts as a child, but as a keen chef I was determined to conquer my dislike and turn it into love. I think it started with this recipe. I like to serve these sprouts with veal or lamb chops, but they're also delicious with grilled fish and lemon.

20 Brussels sprouts, trimmed and halved

3 tablespoons extra virgin olive oil

3 cloves garlic, finely sliced

salt flakes

60 g butter

½ cup (125 ml) pouring cream

freshly ground black pepper

1 bunch chervil, coarsely chopped

Slice Brussels sprouts very finely. Heat half the oil in a large non-stick frying pan over high heat. Add the sprouts and garlic and sauté quickly, stirring occasionally. Add a generous amount of salt and cook for 3–4 minutes or until sprouts are bright green, adding remaining oil if necessary. Add butter, cream and black pepper and stir. Bring to the boil and cook for 3 minutes. Remove from heat, stir in chervil and serve. SERVES 4

> Baked fennel with parmesan, oregano, cream and breadcrumbs

Fennel seems to be one of the most underrated vegetables around, yet it's versatile and delicious. Try this bake with chicken, steak, fish or your favourite roast.

3 medium bulbs fennel, trimmed

50 g unsalted butter

¾ cup (190 ml) pouring cream

1 clove garlic, finely chopped

20 oregano leaves, coarsely chopped

½ cup (35 g) fresh breadcrumbs

40 g grated parmesan

salt flakes and freshly ground black pepper

½ lemon, juiced, to serve

Preheat oven to 175°C. Boil whole fennel bulbs over medium heat in salted water for 25 minutes. Drain and set aside for 10 minutes.

Grease a 30 × 15 cm ovenproof dish. Cut fennel lengthways into 1 cm-thick slices and layer in the dish. Scatter knobs of butter over fennel. Combine cream, garlic and oregano in a small saucepan and bring just to the boil over medium heat. Pour over fennel. Sprinkle breadcrumbs and parmesan over fennel, then season. Cover with foil and bake for 10 minutes. Uncover and bake for a further 10–15 minutes or until golden.

Just before serving, pour lemon juice over fennel. SERVES 4

Twice-cooked green beans in spicy tomato sauce

This dish of green beans, with a sweet-and-sour tomato sauce (or, as the Italians say, agro dolce), goes well with grilled or roasted meats and fish. It can be served hot or cold and works well as part of an antipasto plate.

1½ cups (375 ml) vegetable oil

200 g green beans, topped

50 ml extra virgin olive oil

1 large brown onion, halved and sliced

1 bay leaf

3 cloves garlic, finely sliced

1 small red chilli, finely sliced

2 tablespoons red-wine vinegar

2 tablespoons castor sugar

salt flakes and freshly ground black pepper

1 cup (250 ml) tomato passata

1 handful basil leaves, torn

Heat vegetable oil in a medium saucepan over high heat. When oil is hot, add beans and fry for 2 minutes. Remove and drain on kitchen paper.

Heat olive oil in a heavy-based non-stick frying pan. Add onion, bay leaf, garlic and chilli. Cook over medium heat for about 5 minutes or until onion is translucent. Stir in vinegar, sugar, salt and pepper. Simmer for 30 seconds, add tomato passata and simmer for a further 3 minutes. Add beans to tomato mixture and stir. Stir in basil leaves and serve. SERVES 4

< White winter bake with celeriac, parsnip and kipfler potato Baharat is a blend of cinnamon, black pepper, nutmeg, cloves and ginger. It is available in spice shops or specialty food stores. Serve this bake with roast chicken or lamb, or with braised lentils.

1 celeriac, peeled and cut into batons
  about 1 cm × 6 cm

5 medium parsnips, peeled and cut
  into quarters

10 kipfler potatoes, scrubbed and sliced
  lengthways

10 cloves garlic, unpeeled and bruised

2 pinches baharat (see glossary)

6 sprigs thyme

salt flakes and freshly ground black pepper

½ cup (125 ml) water

Preheat oven to 165°C. Place celeriac, parsnip, potato, garlic, baharat and thyme in a deep baking dish. Season with salt and pepper and toss gently to combine. Add water, cover with foil and roast for 25 minutes. Uncover, toss gently again and roast for a further 20 minutes or until vegetables are golden and cooked.
SERVES 6–8

Brussels sprouts and Dutch carrots with butter and parsley A lot of people overlook Brussels sprouts. The secret is in the butter, the parsley and the carrots that go with them. You could also add peas in the last minute of cooking, if you like. Serve with slow-baked veal shanks, fish or lamb.

16 small Brussels sprouts, trimmed

⅓ cup (80 g) table salt

1 bunch Dutch (baby) carrots, trimmed
  and scrubbed

100 g unsalted butter, chopped

½ bunch flat-leaf parsley, leaves picked
  and finely chopped

salt flakes and freshly ground black pepper

Remove outer and inner leaves from the Brussels sprouts, down to the tightly packed heart. Cut hearts in half and reserve leaves.

Fill a medium-sized saucepan three-quarters full with water and add salt. Bring to the boil over medium heat and add carrots. Boil for 3 minutes, then add Brussels sprouts, leaves and hearts and cook for 3 minutes. Drain vegetables. Add butter, parsley, salt and pepper and toss to combine. Serve immediately.
SERVES 4–6

Braised cannellini beans with green olives, rosemary and peas

This bean dish goes with almost anything. Try serving it alongside veal, pork chops, chicken, braised lamb shanks or a robust roasted fish such as swordfish or snapper, with a buttered spiced rice pilaf.

2½ cups (500 g) cannellini beans, soaked
 in cold water overnight and drained

⅓ cup (80 ml) extra virgin olive oil, plus extra for drizzling

100 g pancetta (see glossary), roughly chopped

5 golden shallots, peeled and sliced

salt flakes and freshly ground black pepper

6 cloves garlic, finely chopped

2 sprigs rosemary, leaves picked and finely chopped

8 pitted green olives, chopped

1 cup (250 ml) chicken stock

1 cup (120 g) frozen peas

Place cannellini beans in a large saucepan of water, bring to the boil then cook over medium heat for 40–50 minutes or until tender. Strain, reserving liquid.

Heat olive oil in a large, heavy-based frying pan over low heat. Add pancetta, shallots, salt, pepper and garlic and stir well. Cook until shallots are soft and caramelised (about 8 minutes). Stir in rosemary and cook for a further 3 minutes. Add drained beans, olives and stock and stir well. Simmer for 15 minutes. If necessary, add some of the reserved cooking liquid from the beans. Add peas and cook for a few more minutes. Check seasoning. Serve with a drizzle of olive oil. SERVES 6

Baked layered potato and Jerusalem artichoke with cream and parmesan This dish is fabulous with roasted meat or poultry.

6 large desiree potatoes, peeled

10 large Jerusalem artichokes, peeled

600 ml chicken stock

400 ml pouring cream

3 sprigs thyme

2 large cloves garlic, peeled and bruised

100 g grated parmesan

100 g butter

salt flakes and freshly ground black pepper

2 pinches nutmeg or baharat (see glossary)

Preheat oven to 170°C. Slice potatoes and artichokes very thinly. Place stock and cream in a saucepan and bring to the boil over medium heat. Remove from heat, stir in thyme and garlic and set aside for 5 minutes. Place a layer of potato, overlapping slightly, on the base of 1 large or 2 medium-sized greased ovenproof dishes and top with a layer of artichokes. Sprinkle with a little parmesan and dot with butter. Continue layering, finishing with a layer of potato, parmesan and butter. Remove thyme and garlic from cream mixture and pour over potatoes. Season, then sprinkle with nutmeg or baharat and scatter with thyme sprigs. Bake for 45 minutes or until cooked and golden.

SERVES 4–6

My mashed potatoes Here's an idea for decadent, velvety mashed potato for 4–6 people. Preheat the oven to 200°C and bake 4 large desiree or bintje potatoes (scrubbed, skin left on and scored around the middle) for 1 hour. Remove from oven and allow to cool for 4 minutes or until just cool enough to handle. Peel immediately, then press through a mouli or potato ricer into a saucepan over low heat. Add a splash of milk and use a wooden spoon to beat in 250 g cold, diced, unsalted butter. Divine.

Lentil and potato braise I had some cotechino sausages on hand – these Italian pork sausages are sticky and rich – and I couldn't decide whether to serve them with lentils or potatoes, so I did both. But any type of pork and veal sausage would go well with this braise.

1½ cups (300 g) Australian puy lentils

½ cup (125 ml) extra virgin olive oil

5 golden shallots, peeled and chopped

1 small red chilli, split lengthways

5 cloves garlic, chopped

2 teaspoons ground fennel seed

1 bay leaf

3 sprigs thyme

3 desiree potatoes, peeled and
   cut into 5 mm-thick slices

1.2 litres chicken or vegetable stock

1 tablespoon sherry vinegar

Place lentils in a saucepan of cold water and bring to the boil over medium heat, then strain. Place a medium-sized, heavy-based saucepan over medium heat and add oil. When oil is hot, add shallots, chilli and garlic and cook for 3–5 minutes. Add ground fennel, bay leaf, thyme and potatoes and fry for 5 minutes. Add lentils and stock, then simmer over low heat for 20–30 minutes or until potatoes are cooked and lentils are very tender. Stir in sherry vinegar and serve. SERVES 6

Sautéed potato and chorizo

This is an easy way to jazz up a barbecued chicken. I also love it with whole snapper stuffed with lemon and oregano, splashed with wine and oil and baked in foil.

½ cup (125 ml) extra virgin olive oil

200 g hot chorizo sausage, chopped

4 cloves garlic, finely sliced

4 golden shallots, halved and sliced

1 teaspoon cayenne pepper

1 teaspoon sweet paprika

2 fresh bay leaves

800 g small desiree potatoes, peeled
  and cut into 5 mm-thick slices

salt flakes and freshly ground black pepper

½ cup (125 ml) white wine

1 cup (250 ml) water

4 sprigs oregano

Heat a little of the oil in a large heavy-based frying pan over medium heat. Add chorizo, garlic, spring onions, cayenne, paprika and bay leaves and stir for 1 minute. Add potato slices and remaining oil and stir. Season to taste and add wine. Bring to the boil, then add water and oregano sprigs. Lower heat and simmer for 15 minutes or until the liquid is almost evaporated and the potatoes are caramelised on the bottom of the pan. Adjust seasoning if necessary and serve. SERVES 4

Waldorf salad This is a modern spin on the classic Waldorf. I've kept the walnuts and apple but added a poached egg, asparagus and crisped pancetta.

16 asparagus spears, trimmed

100 ml extra virgin olive oil

salt flakes and freshly ground black pepper

4 free-range eggs (60 g each)

2 granny smith apples, cored,
  thinly sliced and cut into matchsticks

1 celery heart, finely sliced

½ red onion, finely sliced

1 lemon, juiced

½ bunch chives, finely chopped

½ bunch chervil, chopped

100 g fresh goat's curd (see glossary)

½ cup (50 g) walnuts, toasted, chopped and
  tossed in a little olive oil

8 slices pancetta, roasted at 165°C
  for 5–7 minutes

Cook asparagus for 3–4 minutes in lightly salted boiling water. Drain, then dress immediately with half the olive oil and season. Slide the eggs into a pan of lightly salted boiling water with a splash of vinegar added and poach for 3–5 minutes. Drain and keep warm.

To make the salad, place apples, celery and onion in a bowl. Stir in half the lemon juice, chives and half the chervil, then toss to combine.

To serve, place asparagus on plates, top each pile with a poached egg and spoon apple salad on the side. Place goat's curd on eggs and scatter with walnuts and crumbled pancetta. Sprinkle with remaining chervil, and drizzle with remaining lemon juice and olive oil. Season and serve immediately. SERVES 4

White cabbage, radish, mint and caraway salad
Delicious with fried fish, veal schnitzel or roast pork, this cabbage dish will also liven up a sandwich the next day.

½ white cabbage, very finely shredded

6 sprigs mint, leaves picked and torn

6 red radishes, very finely sliced

½ red onion, finely chopped

1½ teaspoons ground caraway seeds

½ lemon, juiced

100 ml extra virgin olive oil

salt flakes and freshly ground black pepper

Place cabbage, mint, radishes and onion in a large bowl. Combine caraway seeds, lemon juice, olive oil, salt and pepper in a small bowl and whisk until smooth. Add dressing to cabbage and toss lightly to combine. Set aside for 5 minutes before serving. SERVES 6

Boiled potato
You can make a more robust version of this salad by adding boiled potato (peeled and cut into halves or quarters) and stirring through 2–3 tablespoons sour cream. This makes a great match for a spicy beef casserole.

> Italian coleslaw with radish
Radish gives extra bite to this lighter-style coleslaw. It's terrific served on its own or as an accompaniment to pasta or any dish you would pair with traditional coleslaw.

½ Savoy cabbage, very finely shredded

½ white radish (daikon), peeled and shaved into thin ribbons

3 carrots, peeled and shaved into thin ribbons

6 red radishes, finely sliced

½ red onion, finely sliced

100 ml extra virgin olive oil

2 tablespoons red-wine vinegar

salt flakes and freshly ground black pepper

Place all the ingredients in a large bowl. Toss to combine and add seasoning. If you'd like some extra bite, add finely sliced red chillies. Adding shaved apple is another variation, or, for a creamier dressing, use a little sour cream. SERVES 4–6

Spinach and yoghurt salad with lentils This salad is fantastic served with boiled potatoes and fish, lamb chops or grilled or roasted chicken, or just on its own.

½ cup (100 g) Australian puy lentils

1 bay leaf

500 g baby spinach leaves or
   1 bunch young spinach, stems trimmed

1 clove garlic, finely chopped

salt flakes and freshly ground black pepper

1 lemon, juiced

⅓ cup (80 ml) extra virgin olive oil

6 sprigs mint, leaves picked and torn

6 sprigs tarragon, coarsely chopped

6 sprigs dill, coarsely chopped

¾ cup (200 g) plain yoghurt

4 spring onions, sliced diagonally

50 g butter, melted

Cook lentils in boiling water for 1–2 minutes, remove from heat and drain. Place lentils in a small saucepan, cover with cold water and add bay leaf. Bring to the boil over medium heat then simmer for about 10 minutes or until lentils are tender. Drain.

Shred three-quarters of the spinach. Combine shredded spinach, lentils and garlic in a large bowl. Season with salt and pepper. Add lemon juice, oil and herbs and toss gently. Stir through the yoghurt, spring onions, remaining whole spinach leaves and melted butter. Season with pepper and serve. SERVES 6

Herbs Having your own herb garden means salad-making is a dream. You can be much more experimental when fresh herbs are on hand and the difference in flavour is amazing. We bought wine barrels and cut them in half, drilled drainage holes in the base and added potting mix and herb seedlings. In winter, when some of the summer herbs had died back, we planted cos-style lettuces and plucked leaves all the way into spring.

Potato salad with crispy bacon Potato salad is a must on a picnic or at a barbecue. It can feed a lot of hungry mouths and it travels well unrefrigerated. I like to dress the potatoes in a mix of mayonnaise and sour cream – or yoghurt if you prefer a healthier version. Just don't scrimp on the crispy bacon or soft-boiled eggs.

8 medium desiree potatoes,
    cut into 1 cm-thick slices

50 ml extra virgin olive oil

1 red onion, halved and sliced

½ cup (140 g) mayonnaise

½ cup (120 g) sour cream or plain yoghurt

salt flakes and freshly ground black pepper

8 sprigs flat-leaf parsley, coarsely chopped

4 large free-range eggs

½ bunch chives, finely chopped

6 sprigs tarragon, leaves picked and
    coarsely chopped

6 rashers bacon, fried until crisp,
    then broken into pieces

Place potatoes in a saucepan of lightly salted water over medium heat and boil for 15–18 minutes or until tender. Drain. Transfer to a large bowl and drizzle with the olive oil. Set aside to cool for 15 minutes, then add onion.

To make dressing, mix mayonnaise and sour cream in a small bowl. Season well and stir through parsley.

Boil eggs, covered, over medium heat for 6 minutes. Drain and refresh in cold water for 1 minute.

Add mayonnaise dressing, chives and tarragon to potatoes and toss gently to combine, then top with bacon. Slice off the pointy end of the soft-boiled eggs and scoop eggs out onto the salad. Finish with a grind of black pepper and scatter salt flakes over. SERVES 6–8

Warm potato, dill, caper and mustard salad A modern twist on the traditional potato salad, this is a favourite in my repertoire. It's simple and delicious. Remember to dress the potatoes while they are still quite warm, to wilt and absorb the dressing.

8 desiree potatoes (4 peeled, 4 scrubbed)

100 ml extra virgin olive oil

1 tablespoon Dijon mustard

1 tablespoon seeded mustard

4 tablespoons white-wine vinegar

1 lemon, juiced and zested

3 red shallots, peeled and sliced

3 tablespoons tiny capers

2 sprigs dill, chopped

2 sprigs flat-leaf parsley, coarsely chopped

Cut potatoes diagonally into 2 cm-thick slices. Place in a medium-sized saucepan of boiling water and cook over medium heat until tender. Drain well. Mix oil, both mustards, vinegar, lemon juice and zest and shallots in a large bowl. Add hot potatoes and stir to coat. Add capers, dill and parsley and toss gently to combine. Serve warm. SERVES 8

Winter tabbouleh This salad is a little heavier than traditional tabbouleh and the flavours are more intense. You will be surprised by the nutty, unique flavour that cauliflower takes on when roasted. Serve the salad with grilled quail, chicken or fish.

1 cauliflower, broken into florets and stems sliced

¾ cup (120 g) fine burghul (see glossary)

½ bulb fennel, trimmed and finely sliced

1 red onion, finely sliced

½ cup (80 g) blanched almonds, lightly toasted

8 sprigs flat-leaf parsley, chopped

½ cup pomegranate seeds (optional), (see glossary)

dressing

55 ml pomegranate molasses (see glossary)

½ teaspoon salt flakes

1 teaspoon ground cinnamon

1 lemon, juiced

2 teaspoons sugar

100 ml extra virgin olive oil

½ clove garlic, very finely chopped

freshly ground black pepper

Preheat oven to 175°C. Place cauliflower on a lightly greased baking tray and roast for 25 minutes. Set aside to cool.

Place burghul in a small bowl, cover with 1 cup boiling water and leave for 10 minutes or until liquid is absorbed. Use a fork to separate the grains.

To make the dressing, place all ingredients in a small bowl and stir well. Set aside for 5 minutes.

To make the salad, place cauliflower, burghul, fennel, onion, almonds, parsley and pomegranate seeds, if using, in a large bowl. Pour on dressing and toss gently to combine. SERVES 6–8

Beetroot salad with red onion and fetta

This is a wonderfully earthy salad and well worth the mess – beetroot is not the easiest vegetable to handle, but the salad is addictive. Serve it on its own, with seared or crumbed fish, grilled meats or in rolls with pork sausages and lettuce leaves.

5 medium to large beetroot, trimmed

¾ cup (165 g) castor sugar

3 tablespoons salt flakes

150 ml red-wine vinegar

1 red onion, finely sliced

6 sprigs mint, leaves picked

6 sprigs flat-leaf parsley

150 ml extra virgin olive oil

salt flakes and freshly ground black pepper

100 g baby chard or baby spinach leaves (optional)

150 g fetta

Place beetroot in a large saucepan and cover with cold water. Add sugar, salt and half the vinegar and bring to the boil over medium heat. Simmer for 1 hour or until tender, then drain. Leave beetroot until cool enough to handle, then remove skins under cold running water.

Grate beetroot coarsely and place in a large bowl. Add onion, mint leaves, parsley leaves, remaining vinegar and olive oil. Turn gently to combine and season to taste. Place salad in a serving bowl and fold in chard or spinach leaves, if using. Break fetta into small pieces and scatter over salad. SERVES 4

Smoky eggplant salad with walnuts and borlotti beans

Eggplant is always popular. When buying, look for those with firm, shiny, wrinkle-free skin. This salad goes well with spiced lamb, pan-fried snapper or grilled tuna. Or serve it with toasted Turkish bread as part of a mezze plate.

2 large eggplants

350 g fresh borlotti beans, shelled

⅓ cup (80 ml) sherry vinegar

100 ml extra virgin olive oil

1 clove garlic

1½ cups (150 g) walnuts, chopped

salt flakes and freshly ground black pepper

½ bunch coriander, coarsely chopped

½ bunch flat-leaf parsley, finely chopped

5 spring onions, finely sliced

½ red onion, finely chopped

1 tablespoon plain yoghurt

Preheat barbecue to hot. Use a fork to prick eggplants all over. Place on hot grill and cook for 20–30 minutes or until blackened and tender. Alternatively, hold eggplants over a gas flame on the stove for 5 minutes to char the skin, then cook for 25 minutes in an oven preheated to 200°C. When cool enough to handle, scoop out the flesh, drain excess juices and chop, then transfer to a bowl.

Cook borlotti beans in boiling water for 15–20 minutes or until tender. Drain, then dress with vinegar and half the olive oil. Place garlic, half the walnuts and salt in a mortar and pestle and crush to a paste. Stir garlic mixture into eggplant. Add coriander, parsley, spring and red onions, beans and remaining walnuts, and stir through yoghurt. Arrange salad on a platter, drizzle with the remaining olive oil and season. SERVES 4

Greek salad

A great Greek salad is a must-have dish on all my holidays. It complements any barbecue, can be served with fish, lamb or chicken and makes a great picnic option – just fill flat bread with the salad, add a rissole and roll it up.

300 g fetta

½ cup oregano leaves, torn

1 lemon, zested and juiced

200 ml extra virgin olive oil

freshly ground black pepper

1 clove garlic, finely chopped

⅓ cup (80 ml) red-wine vinegar

6–8 tomatoes, sliced

6 Lebanese cucumbers

½ cup finely chopped pickles
   (such as giardiniera or pickled vegetables,
   green banana chillies or dill cucumber)

½ cup (80 g) kalamata olives

½ cup mint leaves, torn

2 red onions, sliced

crusty bread and tzatziki, to serve

Slice fetta into long, thin strips. Place on a plate and sprinkle with oregano and lemon zest. Drizzle with half the olive oil and season with pepper.

To make dressing, whisk together garlic, remaining oil, vinegar and half the lemon juice in a small bowl.

Pour a little of the dressing over tomatoes. Peel three of the cucumbers and slice finely. Toss with remaining dressing. Place pickles, olives, mint, onion and remaining lemon juice in a bowl and stir to combine.

Arrange tomatoes and sliced cucumbers on a platter. Cut remaining cucumbers into long fingers and scatter, along with fetta, on top. Spoon over the pickle mixture. Serve with crusty bread and tzatziki. SERVES 4–6

> Eggplant pickled with red capsicum

This pickled eggplant is really delicious. I consider it an antipasto essential, as it adds a little colour and texture.

2 large eggplants

salt flakes

2 cloves garlic, finely chopped

4 sprigs flat-leaf parsley, leaves picked and torn

1 red capsicum, seeded and very finely chopped

1 red chilli, finely sliced

100 ml red-wine vinegar

100 ml extra virgin olive oil

freshly ground black pepper

Cut eggplants lengthways into thin slices. Blanch eggplant in lightly salted boiling water for 2–3 minutes (you may need to do this in batches). Drain and set aside to cool. Squeeze out excess water and transfer to a large serving bowl. Add garlic, parsley, capsicum, chilli, vinegar and oil and toss gently to combine. Season with salt and pepper. Leave for 10 minutes before serving, to allow flavours to develop. SERVES 4–6

Pickled mushroom salad with sour cream, dill, chilli, parsley and spring onion I was inspired to make this salad by the Russian lady who used to pick mushrooms and sell them to me at the back door of the kitchen at the Melbourne Wine Room. Every time, she would go on about her mother's salad of pickled mushroom with sour cream until finally I came up with a version of my own.

200 ml red-wine vinegar or sherry vinegar

150 g pine mushrooms, trimmed and sliced

100 g cepe or portobello mushrooms, trimmed and sliced

100 g button mushrooms, sliced

2 golden shallots, sliced

2 sprigs dill, chopped

2 spring onions, finely sliced

4 sprigs flat-leaf parsley, chopped, plus extra (optional), to serve

1 small red chilli, finely sliced

1 clove garlic, finely sliced

100 g sour cream

salt flakes and freshly ground black pepper

3 tablespoons extra virgin olive oil

crusty bread, to serve

Pour vinegar or sherry and 200 ml water into a large saucepan. Place over medium heat and bring to the boil. Add all the mushrooms and cook for 4–5 minutes. Drain well and transfer mushrooms to a large serving bowl. Stir in the shallots.

To make the dressing, place dill, spring onions, parsley, chilli, garlic and sour cream in a small bowl and stir well. Pour dressing over mushrooms and stir gently to combine. Season with salt and pepper. Drizzle over olive oil, then scatter with extra parsley, if using, and serve with crusty bread as a starter or as part of an antipasto platter.
SERVES 4

Shaved fennel, ricotta and pea salad I've had to work hard with individuals over the years to convince them to try fennel raw, yet it's an absolutely delicious vegetable. When shaved finely and dressed with extra virgin olive oil and lemon, its delicate anise flavour is seductive. When paired with fresh ricotta, peas and mint, it wins everyone over straightaway. This is the perfect spring salad that you can throw together in minutes.

⅔ cup fresh or frozen green peas

150 ml extra virgin olive oil

salt flakes and freshly ground black pepper

1 large bulb fennel

5–6 sprigs mint, leaves picked and torn

4 tablespoons lemon juice

300 g ricotta

Place peas in lightly salted boiling water and blanch for 15–20 seconds. Drain, then drizzle with a little of the olive oil. Season with salt and pepper to taste.

Cut the fennel in half, reserve green tops and slice bulb very finely. Place fennel, peas, mint and fennel sprigs in a large bowl. Whisk lemon juice and remaining olive oil in a small bowl. Pour over fennel mixture and toss to combine.

To serve, divide ricotta evenly and pile onto plates. Spoon on fennel salad and season generously. SERVES 4

Fennel Don't throw away the soft, furry fronds as these are lovely picked off and scattered over the salad after dressing. When buying fennel, always look for fat, round bulbs that are firm and sweet-smelling. Hopefully, they'll have a little greenery still attached.

Carrot and oregano salad with lentils and red-wine vinegar

The roasted garlic dressing is as luscious as mayonnaise and gives this salad a buttery, nutty flavour. Serve it as part of an antipasto platter, with pasta, or alongside grilled lamb or chicken.

½ cup (100 g) small green or red lentils

1 bunch Dutch (baby) carrots,
    trimmed and peeled

100 ml red-wine vinegar

100 ml extra virgin olive oil

2 bulbs garlic, brushed with olive oil and
    roasted at 150°C for 30 minutes

6 sprigs oregano, leaves picked

salt flakes and freshly ground black pepper

½ red onion, finely chopped

½ bunch flat-leaf parsley, leaves picked

Place lentils in a small saucepan of boiling water, simmer for 10 minutes, then drain.

Slice carrots into thin ribbons. Blanch in boiling water for 15 seconds, then drain.

Combine vinegar and olive oil in a medium bowl. Squeeze in roasted garlic cloves. Add oregano, salt and pepper and whisk well, then add onion and stir. Add carrots and lentils, while still warm, and parsley. Stir to combine. Set aside for 10 minutes before serving, to allow flavours to develop. SERVES 4

> Shaved fennel and artichoke salad

I love this salad because it is fresh and unusual. It matches well with pasta or chargrilled meats, fish or vegetables. It can also be served as a light entrée.

150 ml extra virgin olive oil
    (best quality you can afford)

2 lemons, juiced

salt flakes and freshly ground black pepper

4 prepared artichokes (see note page 76)

1–2 large bulbs fennel, fronds reserved

100 g grated parmigiano reggiano, to serve

Whisk olive oil and lemon juice in a bowl. Season.

Slice artichokes very thinly. Slice fennel, slightly thicker than artichokes. Place artichokes, fennel and reserved fronds in a large bowl. Add dressing and toss to combine. Check seasoning. Sprinkle the parmigiano reggiano over the salad. SERVES 4

Tarragon green bean salad

A warm bean salad with fresh herbs is a brilliant match for barbecued or pan-fried meats. This salad, with chervil and tarragon, is especially delicious.

500 g green beans, topped

1 red onion, finely chopped

2 tablespoons Dijon mustard

2 tablespoons capers, chopped

½ bunch chervil, coarsely chopped

½ bunch French tarragon, leaves picked
   (left whole if small, otherwise chopped)

100 ml extra virgin olive oil

1 clove garlic, finely chopped

salt flakes and freshly ground black pepper

4 tablespoons white-wine vinegar

Cook beans for 4 minutes in lightly salted boiling water. Drain well and keep warm. Place remaining ingredients, except vinegar, in a large bowl and stir to combine. Add beans and toss to coat with dressing. Stir in vinegar and serve immediately.
SERVES 4

Tarragon vinegar

To make tarragon vinegar, drop a few tarragon sprigs into your favourite white-wine or champagne vinegar. Leave to infuse for 10 days, then use it to deglaze the pan after cooking poultry or to dress fresh curd cheese, poached eggs or a green salad.

Pistachio aïoli Aïoli is a garlic mayonnaise
made in the south of France. I like to serve it with
pan-fried snapper, along with witlof, apple and
watercress salad and lemon wedges. I also love it
with pan-fried dory or whiting, or barbecued chicken.

¾ cup (110 g) pistachios, toasted

1 clove garlic, finely chopped

½ cup flat-leaf parsley leaves, chopped

2 tablespoons extra virgin olive oil

½ bulb garlic, roasted at 150°C for 30 minutes

1½ cups (450 g) mayonnaise (see recipe, page 191)

1 lemon, juiced

salt flakes and freshly ground black pepper

Pound pistachios and raw garlic in a mortar and pestle or process in a food processor.
Add parsley and olive oil and pound or process until combined. Transfer to a bowl,
add roasted garlic flesh and stir well. Add mayonnaise and lemon juice and stir. Season.
Pour into a jar and cover closely with plastic film. Aïoli will keep for up to 2 days if
covered and refrigerated. MAKES ABOUT 2 CUPS

Mayonnaise Homemade mayonnaise (page 191)
can transform so many dishes from mundane to more-ish.
Roasted or barbecued lamb or veal chops are a perfect match
for anchoïde (page 192) or pistachio aïoli. For a quick snack,
spread anchoïde over a piece of toasted sourdough bread and
have a little salad on the side. Simple but delicious.

< Traditional mayonnaise This can be kept in the fridge for up to one week. Just before serving, stir through a little yoghurt or sour cream to lighten and add a certain sharpness.

4 egg yolks

1 tablespoon Dijon mustard

2 pinches salt flakes

½ lemon, juiced

3 cups (750 ml) olive oil

Place egg yolks, mustard, salt and lemon juice in a food processor and process until combined. With the motor running, pour in olive oil in a thin, steady stream until smoothly combined and thick. If you prefer, you can use a whisk instead, but make sure you add the oil in a thin, steady stream. Check seasoning.

Add 1–2 teaspoons boiling water to thin if necessary. Pour into a jar, cover closely with plastic film and refrigerate until needed. MAKES ABOUT 2 CUPS

Babaghanoush This Middle-Eastern dip can be made with or without the smoky flavour – it's up to you. For a subtle smoky taste, char the eggplant skin on the barbecue before baking.

4 medium to large eggplants

2 cloves garlic, chopped

1 lemon, juiced

150 ml extra virgin olive oil

100 ml tahini (see glossary)

salt flakes and freshly ground black pepper

¾ cup (200 g) plain yoghurt

1 tablespoon extra virgin olive oil, extra

1 tablespoon chopped mint, to serve

Preheat oven to 180°C. Rotate eggplants over a gas flame or barbecue on a hot grill for 4–6 minutes to blacken the skin. Place on a baking tray and bake for 15–20 minutes or until eggplants are very soft.

Leave eggplants until cool enough to handle, then halve and scrape flesh into a food processor, discarding skins. Process briefly, then add garlic, lemon juice, olive oil and tahini and process until smooth. Check seasoning. When completely cool, fold in yoghurt. Serve drizzled with extra olive oil and scattered with fresh mint. MAKES ABOUT 6 CUPS

Babaghanoush You don't have to serve these recipes as dips. The babaghanoush can be stirred through Napoli sauce for pasta with a difference, served with seared yellowfin tuna and a tomato salad or accompanied by fried haloumi cheese and a squeeze of lemon.

Zhoug

This spicy condiment (pronounced 'zoog', with a short vowel, like 'look') can be eaten with bread, drizzled over baked cheese pastries or served with barbecued meat, seafood or poultry. It is especially delicious with seared sardines or grilled chicken with yoghurt.

1½ bunches coriander

8 small red chillies, chopped

1 tablespoon chopped preserved lemon rind

3 cloves garlic, chopped

1 bunch flat-leaf parsley

2 teaspoons ground cumin

1 teaspoon ground caraway seeds

3 cardamom pods, seeds removed
    from husk and crushed

200 ml extra virgin olive oil

1 teaspoon freshly ground black pepper

1 teaspoon salt flakes

50 ml water

Combine all ingredients in a mortar and pestle or food processor and pound or process until smooth. Add a little more olive oil to thin if necessary.
MAKES ABOUT 1½ CUPS

Herb dressing

Dragoncello is another quick herb dressing that is wonderful when drizzled over grilled tuna, scallops, lamb or steak. Blanch equal parts flat-leaf parsley, tarragon and oregano in boiling water, refresh in cold water and squeeze dry. Put in a food processor and process with sliced red chilli, chopped garlic, salt flakes and extra virgin olive oil to make a thick green oil.

> # Anchoïde

I've been known to enjoy this simply smothered over crusty bread or bruschetta, but you might like to try serving it with roasted veal fillet, watercress salad and lemon wedges or spread over chargrilled tuna or marlin.

150 g canned tuna in oil, drained

4 anchovy fillets

2 tablespoons capers

1 bulb garlic, roasted at 150°C for 30 minutes

2 small red chillies, very finely chopped

freshly ground black pepper

1 tablespoon cold water

1½ cups (450 g) mayonnaise (see recipe, page 191)

Place tuna, anchovies, capers, roasted garlic flesh, chillies and pepper in a food processor. Add water and process until you have a smooth paste.

Add mayonnaise and process again until smooth.
Pour into a jar and cover closely with plastic film and keep, refrigerated, for up to 2 days. MAKES ABOUT 2 CUPS

Tzatziki The summery cucumber and mint flavours become more pronounced the longer you leave this dish to sit. I always buy European or Greek yoghurt for this dip. If neither is available, use plain yoghurt but drain it through a cloth for a couple of hours until the consistency thickens.

3 Lebanese cucumbers

½ clove garlic, finely chopped

4 sprigs mint, leaves picked and finely chopped

2 sprigs dill, finely chopped

100 ml extra virgin olive oil

salt flakes and freshly ground black pepper

250 g Greek-style thick yoghurt

Coarsely grate cucumbers and gently squeeze out excess moisture. Combine in a large bowl with garlic, mint, dill and half the oil. Season, then fold in yoghurt. Place in refrigerator for at least a couple of hours to let the flavours develop.

To serve, stir again, pile into a bowl and drizzle with remaining olive oil. MAKES ABOUT 3 CUPS

Tzatziki Try with roast chicken or grilled fish, or serve with pan-fried calamari, rocket and lemon. It's also delicious as a creamy dressing for Greek salad.

> **Harissa** Spread this on a slice of sourdough, dollop on grilled tuna or any other fish or meat, or use in sandwiches. Refrigerate straightaway, as the tomato won't keep if not chilled. The harissa will then last 3–4 days.

1 bulb garlic

1 large red capsicum

10 large red chillies

1 tablespoon cumin seeds

3 teaspoons caraway seeds

150 ml tomato passata

5 pinches salt flakes

2 teaspoons castor sugar

½ cup (125 ml) olive oil

Preheat oven to 160°C. Place garlic, capsicum and chillies in a baking dish and roast for 20 minutes. Remove chillies, place in a bowl, cover with plastic film and leave for 10 minutes. Continue roasting garlic and capsicum for a further 10 minutes. Place capsicum in a bowl, cover with plastic film and leave for 10 minutes. Remove seeds and skin from chillies and capsicum.

Heat a frying pan over high heat. Add cumin and caraway seeds and toast for 2 minutes. Grind the seeds in a mortar and pestle.

Squeeze garlic pulp out of skins and combine with capsicum, chilli, cumin, caraway, tomato passata, salt, sugar and olive oil in a food processor or blender and process until smooth. The harissa will keep, covered, in the fridge for 3–4 days.

You can use store-bought harissa in the recipes in this book, but be careful to check the heat factor. My fresh harissa is not too hot and has a subtle, sweet spiciness. MAKES ABOUT 1 CUP

Ends

As I've said, I do love the beginning, but let's not dismiss a pure, cleansing finish to a meal, or that last morsel of indulgence. I prefer my desserts and cakes to be full-flavoured and intense, and my fruit-based desserts to be seasonal (there's that word again), with the fruit character pronounced and unmasked.

These recipes are clear, precise, easy to make and present plenty of tips for a professional touch without too much fuss: classic biscuits and tarts; baked goat's curd cheesecake; citrus and melon salads; simple cakes; pannacotta and fruit jellies. Don't confine all these dishes to dessert; many are just as suitable for afternoon tea, or any time you like.

Not all these recipes rely on seasonal ingredients; a lemon cheesecake will almost certainly taste better with fruit from your own tree but fresh, quality produce will also work well. However, with fruits like figs, strawberries, melon and stone fruits, please wait. Understanding how to shop for and select produce is as important as understanding how to prepare and cook it. Seek out produce that looks alive and colourful, not limp and pallid; taste it if you can. If you can't find the right ingredient, improvise or cook something else. Trust your instinct, your eyes and your palate – they will reward you.

Cherry and watermelon salad with rosewater and yoghurt semifreddo

Every year I eagerly await cherry season. Cherries are one of my all-time favourite fruits. Look for the plumpest, darkest fruit.

rosewater and yoghurt semifreddo

140 g castor sugar

2–3 tablespoons water

2 large egg whites

1 cup (250 ml) pouring cream, whipped

500 g plain yoghurt

2 tablespoons lemon juice

cherry and watermelon salad

800 g large cherries, pitted

200 g castor sugar

150 ml balsamic vinegar

1 drop bitter almond essence

½ teaspoon rosewater

¼ watermelon, rind and pips removed

Iranian fairy floss, (optional), to serve
   (available from selected delicatessens
   and food halls)

To make the semifreddo, stir sugar and water in a small saucepan over low heat until sugar dissolves. Increase heat and boil until mixture reaches soft-ball stage (116°C). Place egg whites into the bowl of an electric mixer and beat at high speed until soft peaks form. Pour sugar mixture into egg whites in a thin, steady stream and continue beating until mixture is very thick (about 6 minutes). Set aside to cool.

Line a 1.5–2 litre terrine mould with plastic wrap or baking paper. Combine cream, yoghurt and lemon juice in a bowl and fold into meringue mixture, then spoon into the mould. Freeze for 8 hours or until firm.

For the salad, combine cherries, sugar and balsamic vinegar in a large saucepan over high heat. Cover and cook for 3 minutes. Stir and cook for a further 2 minutes. Transfer to a bowl, add almond essence and rosewater and stir gently.

Cut watermelon into chunky batons. To serve, unmould the semifreddo, slice thickly and place on chilled plates. Arrange watermelon on top, then spoon cherries and juice over. Decorate with Iranian fairy floss, if desired. SERVES 8

Cherries

Cherries cooked in balsamic vinegar are delicious served with chocolate ice-cream, chocolate cake, vanilla pannacotta or stirred through a trifle. The semifreddo could easily be jazzed up by stirring crushed praline, chocolate, rum and raisins or honeycomb through it.

Cherries and raspberries marinated in rosé champagne with pistachio savoiardi

600 g black cherries, stems removed, pitted

200 g castor sugar

½ large lemon, zested and juiced

2 tablespoons balsamic vinegar

½ vanilla bean

1 × 750 ml bottle rosé champagne

2 punnets raspberries

vanilla ice-cream, to serve

pistachio savoiardi

3 eggs, separated

70 g castor sugar, plus extra, for sprinkling

25 g icing sugar, sifted

70 g plain flour, sifted

⅔ cup (100 g) pistachios, finely chopped

To make the savoiardi, preheat oven to 175°C. Grease and line a baking tray with baking paper. Place egg yolks and castor sugar in a medium-sized bowl and beat with a hand-held electric mixer until pale and thick. In a separate bowl, beat egg whites with electric mixer until soft peaks form. Sprinkle with icing sugar and beat until firm. Fold half the flour into the egg-yolk mixture, then fold in half the egg white mixture. Add remaining flour, mix well and fold in remaining egg white mixture.

Fit a 2 cm plain nozzle to a piping bag and pipe mixture in 5 cm lengths on the prepared baking tray. Sprinkle with extra castor sugar and pistachios. Bake for 10–15 minutes or until pale golden. (Makes 40–45 biscuits, so you will need to do several batches.)

Place cherries, sugar, lemon zest, vinegar and vanilla bean in a large heavy-based saucepan. Cook over high heat for 3–4 minutes until cherries start to release their juice. Pour the fruit into a bowl and set aside. When cool, add lemon juice, a third of the champagne, and raspberries. Stir and set aside for 5–10 minutes.

To serve, place small scoops of ice-cream in chilled serving glasses or bowls and spoon over berry mixture. Top up glasses with champagne and serve with pistachio savoiardi on the side.

SERVES 8

> # Melon salad with lime, vanilla and mint
This salad is simple and refreshing but it does rely on your sourcing the sweetest, ripest melons. The syrup can be made ahead and warmed through with the mint at the last minute.

250 g castor sugar

50 ml water

2 limes, zested and juiced

1 vanilla bean, split

1 lemon, juiced

½ bunch mint or lemon verbena, leaves picked

½ rockmelon, peeled, seeded and chilled

½ honeydew melon, peeled, seeded and chilled

¼ watermelon, rind removed and chilled

10 lychees, peeled

Combine sugar and water in a medium-sized saucepan and add lime zest and vanilla bean. Stir over low heat until sugar dissolves, then bring to a simmer. Remove from heat and stir in lime and lemon juices. Leave to cool, then stir in mint or lemon verbena leaves.

Cut rockmelon and honeydew into very thin slices and arrange in a large, shallow serving bowl. Cut watermelon into thin triangles and add to bowl with lychees. Pour sugar syrup over fruit and set aside for 15 minutes before serving.

SERVES 4–6

Syrup The sugar syrup can be infused with herbs such as basil or lemon verbena and used in cocktails or drizzled over berries served with lemon sorbet.

Champagne jelly with grapes, ricotta and crushed amaretti

Champagne jelly is a quick, luscious autumn dessert that is not too sweet or rich. If you like, you can substitute a dessert wine for the champagne, but you'll need to reduce the amount of sugar to your taste.

5½ leaves gold-strength gelatine (see glossary)

600 ml champagne or sparkling wine

4½ tablespoons castor sugar

160 g small seedless red grapes, sliced

8 amaretti biscuits, coarsely crushed, to serve

whipped ricotta

250 g ricotta

2 tablespoons castor sugar

½ lemon, zested and juiced

Soak gelatine in a small amount of cold water until soft. Combine champagne and sugar in a medium-sized saucepan and stir over low heat until sugar dissolves. Squeeze water from gelatine. Add gelatine to wine mixture and stir until dissolved. Strain through a fine sieve placed over a bowl.

Place grapes in the base of 8 × 100 ml moulds and divide champagne mixture evenly between moulds. Cover and transfer to the fridge for 2–4 hours or until set.

To make the whipped ricotta, combine ricotta, sugar and lemon juice and zest in a food processor and blend until smooth.

When jellies are set, unmould onto plates. (To unmould, dip each mould into boiling-hot water for 5 seconds, shake gently and turn over.) Serve with a scoop of whipped ricotta and scatter crushed amaretti biscuits on top. SERVES 8

Poached prunes with yoghurt and brown-sugar caramel

These prunes are lovely warm or cold. For a subtle but delicious variation, poach in jasmine tea instead of Earl Grey. I like to use sheep's milk yoghurt, which is a bit denser in texture and flavour than the cow's milk variety. It's not hard to find – you can even buy it from many supermarkets.

500 g sheep's milk yoghurt

1⅓ cups (295 g) castor sugar

300 ml water

200 ml red wine

1 cinnamon stick

4 cloves

4 allspice berries

5 black peppercorns

1 orange, zested

4 Earl Grey tea bags

1½ cups (255 g) pitted prunes, soaked in boiling water
   for 25 minutes, drained

3 tablespoons brown sugar

To drain yoghurt, place it in a fine strainer over a bowl and transfer to fridge for 30 minutes.

Combine sugar, water, wine, cinnamon, cloves, allspice, peppercorns and orange zest in a medium-sized saucepan over medium heat. Add tea bags, bring to the boil and simmer for 5 minutes. Stir in prunes and simmer for 10 minutes or until prunes are plump.

Remove prunes from liquid and set aside. Increase heat to high and simmer liquid for 3–5 minutes or until it thickens and reduces. Strain and discard spices and tea bags.

Stir brown sugar into yoghurt and mix well. To serve, place a generous scoop of yoghurt in each bowl and top with warm prunes and syrup. SERVES 6

Strawberries with basil and balsamic

Yes, balsamic works in sweet dishes. It brings out the flavour of the strawberries and marries them beautifully with the basil.

2 punnets strawberries, hulled

½ lemon, juiced

2 tablespoons castor sugar

6 basil leaves, finely shredded

100 ml balsamic vinegar

vanilla ice-cream, to serve

Slice strawberries lengthways and place in a ceramic or stainless-steel bowl. Add lemon juice, sugar, basil leaves and vinegar and toss gently to combine. Set aside for 10 minutes to allow the flavours to develop.

To serve, spoon the marinated strawberries and syrup over vanilla ice-cream, pannacotta (see recipe, page 209) or pavlova. They are particularly sublime with lemon tart. SERVES 4

Cinnamon and vanilla pannacotta with warm spiced pears

Creamy pannacotta is a deliciously modern dessert. Make it the night before serving so it has time to set. Any leftover spiced pears can be served, hot or cold, with your morning muesli or porridge and yoghurt.

1½ cups (375 ml) pouring cream

¾ cup (190 ml) milk

⅓ cup (70 g) castor sugar

1 vanilla bean, split

1 cinnamon stick

2 × 5 g leaves gelatine (gold strength, see glossary)

spiced pears

3 cups (750 ml) red wine

1 cinnamon stick

2 cloves

1 vanilla bean, split

1¼ cups (280 g) castor sugar

rind of 1 orange

1 cup (80 g) frozen or fresh raspberries or blackberries

5 firm pears

To make pannacotta, combine cream, milk and sugar in a medium-sized saucepan over low heat. Stir until sugar dissolves and the mixture is almost boiling. Remove from heat, then stir in vanilla bean and cinnamon. Set aside for 15 minutes. Soak gelatine in a small amount of cold water until soft. Squeeze water from gelatine. Add gelatine to cream mixture and stir until gelatine dissolves. Strain mixture and pour into 4 × 150 ml moulds. Cover and refrigerate for 6 hours or until set.

For the spiced pears, place wine, spices, vanilla bean, sugar, orange rind and berries in a large saucepan over medium heat. Bring to the boil, simmer for 15 minutes, then remove from heat. Peel pears, core and cut into six wedges each. Place pears in the syrup, cover and simmer over low heat for 15 minutes or until tender.

When pannacotta is set, unmould onto plates. (To unmould dip each mould into warm water for a few seconds. Shake gently and turn over.) Serve with warm spiced pears and syrup. SERVES 4

Gelatine leaves In the pannacotta, use gelatine leaves or 'sheets' instead of gelatine powder. They can be purchased from good delis, and give a more consistent result.

Soft meringue with vanilla mascarpone and passionfruit curd

The passionfruit can be replaced with freshly squeezed lime, blood orange or pomegranate juice – all are delicious. The curd will keep in the fridge for up to 10 days.

4 egg whites

175 g castor sugar

1 teaspoon vanilla extract,
   plus 2–3 drops extra

1 teaspoon white-wine vinegar

1 teaspoon cornflour

icing sugar, for dusting

200 g mascarpone

pulp of 2 passionfruit

passionfruit curd

5 egg yolks

⅔ cup (150 g) castor sugar

200 ml strained passionfruit pulp

2 lemons, juiced

70 g soft butter, chopped

Preheat oven to 160°C. Lightly grease a 32 × 24 cm baking dish and line base with baking paper.

To make passionfruit curd, place egg yolks and sugar in a bowl over a saucepan of simmering water and whisk for 5 minutes or until thick. Pour in passionfruit and lemon juices and whisk for a further 5 minutes or until mixture coats the back of a wooden spoon. Remove from heat. Leave the mixture to cool slightly, then whisk in butter. Transfer to a clean bowl, cover and place in fridge for 40 minutes.

To make meringue, whisk egg whites in a large bowl until soft peaks form. Gradually beat in castor sugar, beating until thick and glossy. Add vanilla, vinegar and cornflour and beat until well combined. Spread meringue in prepared baking dish and bake for 20 minutes. Remove from oven, allow to cool a little, then carefully turn out onto a clean, dry tea towel dusted with icing sugar. Leave to cool for 10 minutes.

Place mascarpone and extra vanilla in a bowl and beat until smooth. Spread vanilla mascarpone and one third of the passionfruit curd over meringue and carefully roll lengthways into a Swiss roll. Spread the outside with curd and drizzle with passionfruit pulp. Serve immediately with extra curd, if desired. SERVES 8

Dark chocolate mousse

This is quite a dense, decadent, fudge-like mousse. Go all out on the chocolate – the better the quality, the better the mousse. No one should ever scrimp on chocolate!

300 g dark couverture chocolate, chopped

150 g soft butter

6 eggs, separated

3 tablespoons white rum

40 g castor sugar

140 ml pouring cream, whipped until soft peaks form and chilled

dark couverture chocolate and cocoa powder, to serve

Melt chocolate in a large heatproof bowl placed over a saucepan of simmering water – don't allow the bowl to touch the water. Remove chocolate from heat, stir in butter, egg yolks and rum and set aside to cool for 5 minutes.

Use a hand-beater to whisk egg whites until soft peaks form. Add sugar and whisk again until well combined. Pour cream into chocolate mixture and stir. Gently fold egg whites into chocolate mixture until smooth. Pour into 6 × 250 ml moulds or serving glasses. Cover and chill for a few hours or overnight. Serve with dark chocolate shavings and a good dusting of cocoa. SERVES 6–8

Honey dumpling doughnuts with rosewater and pistachio

This doughnut recipe is great when you need an informal dessert that is easy to pile up on a large plate and offer around. The doughnuts will keep for a couple of days in a sealed container in the pantry. Reheat in a 180°C oven for a few minutes, then drizzle with the syrup.

1 teaspoon (5 g) dried yeast

75 ml warm water

¼ cup (55 g) castor sugar

400 ml milk

60 g butter

pinch of table salt

3 eggs

4 cups (600 g) plain flour, sifted

vegetable oil, for deep-frying

⅓ cup (50 g) shelled pistachios, crushed

⅓ cup (50 g) pine nuts, crushed

ricotta, to serve

rose petals (optional), to serve

honey syrup

375 g honey

¾ cup (190 ml) water

1¾ cups (385 g) castor sugar

2 cinnamon sticks

2 cloves

1 tablespoon rosewater (optional)

To make doughnuts, combine yeast, water and a pinch of the sugar in a small bowl and stir until yeast dissolves. Place milk in a small saucepan over medium heat and bring just to the boil. Remove from heat. Place butter, remaining sugar and salt in a large bowl and add hot milk. Whisk until smooth, then set aside and leave until warm.

Whisk eggs in a bowl until light and frothy. Add eggs, yeast mixture and flour to warm milk mixture. Mix with a wooden spoon until smooth. Cover with plastic film and set aside at room temperature for 1 hour.

To make honey syrup, place all ingredients in a medium-sized saucepan and stir over low heat until sugar dissolves. Bring syrup to the boil and simmer for 5 minutes, skimming any froth from the top. Cool, strain and add rosewater, if you like.

Heat vegetable oil in a large saucepan over medium heat until hot (about 175°C). Drop heaped teaspoons of doughnut mixture into oil and fry until puffed and golden. Remove with a slotted spoon and drain well on kitchen paper. To serve, pour warm honey syrup over doughnuts, sprinkle with nuts and add a dollop of ricotta. Sprinkle with rose petals (optional). SERVES 8–10

Sticky prune pudding with spiced caramel sauce

This prune pudding is a sophisticated alternative to the standard sticky date pudding. You can, of course, substitute pitted dates for the prunes. If you do this, omit the cocoa powder and increase the flour to 300 g.

1⅓ cups (225 g) pitted prunes

450 ml water

1 teaspoon bicarbonate of soda

90 g soft unsalted butter

1 cup (220 g) castor sugar

3 eggs

1½ cups (225 g) self-raising flour

5 tablespoons cocoa powder

½ teaspoon ground cinnamon

½ teaspoon ground cardamom

1 teaspoon vanilla extract

vanilla ice-cream, to serve

spiced caramel sauce

¾ cup (165 g) brown sugar

1 cup (250 ml) pouring cream

180 g unsalted butter

1 cinnamon stick

3 cardamom pods, crushed

2 teaspoons ground ginger

pinch saffron threads, optional

Preheat oven to 180°C. Grease a 20 × 26 cm cake tin and line with baking paper. Place prunes and water in a small saucepan. Bring to the boil over medium heat, then simmer for 10 minutes or until prunes are very soft. Add bicarbonate of soda and stir. Set aside to cool.

Place butter and sugar in a bowl and beat with an electric mixer until pale and thick. Add eggs, one at a time, beating well after each addition. Sift flour, cocoa and spices together and stir well into butter mixture. Add vanilla and prune mixture and stir again.

Pour pudding mixture into prepared tin. Bake for 30–40 minutes or until cooked when tested with a skewer. To make the sauce, combine all ingredients in a small saucepan and bring to the boil over medium heat. Simmer for 2 minutes. Remove from heat and set aside for 5 minutes, then strain into a jug. Serve warm.

Serve pudding warm, topped with vanilla ice-cream and spiced caramel sauce.

SERVES 8

Rhubarb and raspberry crumble with nuts

This crumble is a modern take on my mother's time-tested recipe. The topping is just as delicious baked over poached apple and berries, if you'd prefer.

450 g castor sugar

1 cup (250 ml) water

½ vanilla bean, split

½ lemon, finely zested

2 bunches thick-stemmed rhubarb,
   trimmed and cut into 3–4 cm lengths

300 g frozen raspberries

80 g soft butter

120 g plain flour

100 g brown sugar

50 g ground almonds

½ cup (80 g) cashews, coarsely chopped

1 teaspoon ground cinnamon

1 teaspoon baking powder

clotted cream or vanilla ice-cream, to serve

Preheat oven to 220°C. Combine castor sugar, water, vanilla bean and lemon zest in a large saucepan and bring to the boil. Simmer over medium heat for 2 minutes. Add rhubarb and simmer very gently over low heat (do not boil), uncovered, for 10 minutes. Drain rhubarb. Spoon the rhubarb and half the raspberries into a lightly greased medium-sized ovenproof dish.

To make the crumble, rub butter into flour in a bowl until mixture resembles coarse breadcrumbs. Add brown sugar, almonds, cashews, cinnamon and baking powder and stir well.

Spoon crumble mixture over fruit and scatter over remaining raspberries. Bake for 20–25 minutes or until golden.

Serve crumble with clotted cream or vanilla ice-cream. SERVES 4–6

< Apple strudel with marmalade and currants One afternoon I looked into the fruit bowl and the pickings were slim. I decided to make a strudel from the apples I had and what I could find in the cupboard. This recipe was the result. The strudel is perfect with cream for afternoon tea – the dusting of icing sugar adds a professional touch.

7 large apples, cored and very thinly sliced

1 lemon, zested and juiced

1 orange, zested and juiced

250 g brown sugar

1 tablespoon ground cinnamon

1⅓ cups (200 g) currants, soaked in 250 ml
    boiling water for 10 minutes

⅓ cup (75 g) crystallised ginger, chopped

125 g butter, chopped

12 sheets filo pastry

125 g butter, melted

200 g marmalade

icing sugar, for dusting

pouring cream, to serve

Preheat oven to 180°C. Lightly grease a baking tray. Place apple slices, lemon and orange zest and juices, brown sugar, cinnamon, drained currants, crystallised ginger and butter in a large bowl. Stir well and set aside for 10–15 minutes.

Place 2 sheets filo pastry, overlapping by one-third, on a lightly floured work surface. Brush with melted butter and top with 2 more sheets of pastry. Repeat process twice more; you should now have 4 layers (8 sheets) of pastry.

Spoon half the apple mixture over the pastry. Lay 2 sheets of pastry on top of apple and brush with melted butter. Add another 2 sheets, brush with butter, spread marmalade over pastry and spoon remaining apple mixture on top. Roll pastry into a long log. Carefully lift onto greased tray and form into a horseshoe shape. Brush top with melted butter.

Bake the strudel for 40 minutes or until the pastry is golden and the apples are cooked. Set aside until cool. Dust with icing sugar and serve with cream. SERVES 10–12

Tutti-frutti pudding The old-fashioned lemon delicious gets a makeover. You can quickly throw this self-saucer together, then bang it in the oven and forget about it.

1 lemon, zested and juiced

1 orange, zested and juiced

1 lime, zested and juiced

1½ tangelos, zested

90 g butter

330 g castor sugar

3 eggs, separated

4 tablespoons self-raising flour

315 ml milk

cream or ice-cream, to serve

Preheat oven to 180°C. Place half of each quantity of lemon, orange and lime zests and all the tangelo zest in a small bowl. Discard remaining zest.

Place butter, zests and sugar in a food processor and process until well mixed. Add egg yolks and process until smooth. Combine fruit juices. Add flour, milk and 165 ml of juice to butter mixture and process until smooth. Transfer to a bowl.

In the bowl of an electric mixer, beat egg whites until firm peaks form. Fold egg whites into butter mixture. Pour pudding mixture into a greased 6-cup-capacity ovenproof dish. Place dish in a large baking tray and pour in enough water to come halfway up the sides of dish. Bake for 40–50 minutes or until cooked and golden. Serve with cream or ice-cream. SERVES 4–6

Karen's panforte This is my take on the classic Italian fruitcake from Siena, though it's much chewier than the original. It will keep in an airtight container for a couple of weeks – if you can stop yourself nibbling. I suggest you only make it if you have a sugar thermometer to ensure a perfect result.

¾ cup (110 g) skinned roasted hazelnuts

⅔ cup (110 g) skinned roasted almonds

⅓ cup (50 g) pistachios

70 g plain flour

1 teaspoon ground cinnamon

1 teaspoon ground ginger

1 teaspoon ground fennel

1 teaspoon ground white pepper

50 g cocoa powder

140 g candied or dried fruit
   (sultanas, apricots, etc.)

180 g dried figs, sliced

140 g honey

200 g castor sugar

Preheat oven to 125°C. Grease a 15 cm square cake tin and line with baking paper. Place hazelnuts, almonds and pistachios in a food processor and pulse until coarsely chopped. Sift combined flour, cinnamon, ginger, fennel, white pepper and cocoa into a bowl and add nuts and fruit.

Place honey and sugar in a medium-sized, heavy-based saucepan over medium heat. Heat honey mixture to 120°C on a sugar thermometer, then pour into dry ingredients and mix well. Spoon mixture into the prepared tin and smooth the top with the back of a spoon. Bake for 10 minutes. Remove from oven and set aside for at least 3 hours. When completely cool, cut panforte into thin slices using a finely serrated knife. MAKES ABOUT 40 SLICES

Baked mascarpone, fig and blackberry tart

Baked mascarpone, fig and blackberry tart If you like figs, make the most of them when they are in season because you never know how long they will be around.

pastry

125 g soft unsalted butter

125 g castor sugar

1 egg, at room temperature

1½ cups (225 g) plain flour

filling

200 g mascarpone

250 g ricotta

100 g castor sugar

100 g honey

1 teaspoon vanilla extract

2 eggs

1 egg yolk

1 tablespoon plain flour

4 large ripe figs, sliced

2 tablespoons apricot jam

1 punnet (150 g) blackberries

100 g castor sugar, extra

½ lemon, juiced

To make the pastry, beat butter and sugar with an electric mixer until thick and pale. Add egg and stir to combine. Fold flour into egg mixture. Turn dough out onto a lightly floured work surface. Shape into a log, cover with plastic film and place in the fridge for 40 minutes.

Lightly grease a round 23 cm tart tin with removable base. Roll out pastry on a lightly floured surface. Lift the pastry into the tin and press lightly. Cover and place in the fridge for 30 minutes. Preheat oven to 180°C. To bake blind, line pastry with baking paper and fill with dried beans or rice. Bake for 10 minutes. Remove paper and beans and bake for a further 10–15 minutes or until pastry is crisp and golden. Set aside to cool. Lower oven temperature to 160°C.

To make filling, combine mascarpone, ricotta, sugar, honey, vanilla, eggs, egg yolk and flour in a food processor and blend until smooth. Pour into cooled tart shell. Arrange sliced figs on top. Bake for 30–40 minutes or until filling is still wobbly and slightly golden.

Place the jam in a small saucepan over medium heat and warm for 1½ minutes. Brush over the tart. Combine blackberries, extra sugar and lemon juice, spoon over the tart and serve. SERVES 6–8

Chocolate chips For a change, drop some chocolate chips into the base just before adding the filling, and then top with chopped macerated prunes or sautéed, caramelised pear slices instead of the figs.

Winter fruit compote pie
This is a cross between a pie and a pudding. Any of your favourite fruits, such as berries, can be substituted.

4 slices fresh pineapple, peeled,
    cored and quartered

2 small pears, peeled,
    cored and cut into six pieces

2 small apples, peeled,
    cored and cut into six pieces

4 thick sticks rhubarb, trimmed and
    cut into 4 cm pieces

250 g castor sugar

½ vanilla bean, split

1 lemon, zested

1 cinnamon stick

topping

100 g soft butter

150 g castor sugar

1 egg

1 teaspoon vanilla extract

280 g self-raising flour

3 teaspoons ground ginger

pinch of table salt

1 cup (250 ml) milk

sifted icing sugar (optional), to serve

Preheat oven to 180°C. Place pineapple, pear, apple and rhubarb in a large bowl. Add sugar, vanilla bean, lemon zest and cinnamon and mix well. Transfer fruit to an ovenproof dish and bake for 40 minutes or until fruit is cooked. Strain fruit, reserving the juice. Put juice in a small saucepan over medium heat and cook until thickened and reduced by half. Spoon fruit into a large pie dish and pour over reduced juice.

To make the topping, beat butter and sugar until light and creamy. Beat in egg and vanilla until combined. Sift together flour, ginger and salt, then fold half the flour mixture into the butter mixture. Stir in milk, then the remaining flour mixture. Spoon batter over fruit and bake for 25–35 minutes or until golden and cooked. Serve hot or warm, dusted with icing sugar, if you like. SERVES 4–6

Winter peach and apricot tarts

These tarts are delicious served with the best-quality vanilla ice-cream you can find. To top them off, drizzle with a little of the poaching syrup.

400 g dried peaches and apricots

200 g castor sugar

1 cup (250 ml) water

1 lemon, zested and juiced

1 vanilla bean

10 lemon verbena leaves (optional)

2 frozen puff-pastry sheets, thawed

1 egg, lightly beaten

icing sugar, for dusting

vanilla ice-cream, to serve

Place dried fruit in a bowl, pour over boiling water to cover, and soak for 2 hours. Place sugar, water, lemon zest and juice, vanilla bean and verbena leaves (if using) in a saucepan. Bring to the boil over medium heat, add drained fruit, cover and poach for 15–20 minutes or until tender.

Preheat oven to 200°C. Divide one pastry sheet into 4 squares. Cut 4 × 1.5cm-thick frames from the second sheet, brush with egg and place on top of pastry squares. Prick the centre of each pastry with a fork and place on a lightly greased non-stick baking tray. Drain fruit and reserve poaching liquid, discarding vanilla bean and verbena leaves. Arrange fruit on top of pastry. Bake for 12–15 minutes or until pastry is golden and cooked. Remove from oven, dust edges with icing sugar and return to oven for 3–5 minutes to glaze. Serve with ice-cream and a drizzle of poaching syrup. SERVES 4

Fruits In summer you can use fresh, ripe peaches, nectarines, plums or figs instead of the dried fruits in this recipe. There is no need to poach the fresh fruit – just slice thinly, toss with sugar and lemon juice, place on the pastry and bake.

> # Baked lemon and goat's curd cheesecake with pistachios I love a good cheesecake. This one is simple to whip up and delicious served chilled or at room temperature.

base

250 g shortbread biscuits

⅓ cup (50 g) pistachios

40 g butter

filling

300 g ricotta

200 g cream cheese

200 g fresh goat's curd (see glossary)

1 cup (220 g) castor sugar

2 teaspoons grated lemon zest

½ lemon, juiced

1 teaspoon vanilla extract

3 eggs

border

3 tablespoons apricot jam, warmed

¾ cup (110 g) pistachios, chopped

Preheat oven to 140°C. Grease and line a 20 cm spring-form cake tin. To make the base, place biscuits, pistachios and butter in a food processor and pulse until mixture resembles coarse breadcrumbs. Press mixture into the base of the cake tin.

To make the filling, combine cheeses, sugar, lemon zest, juice and vanilla extract in a food processor and blend. Add eggs and process until smooth. Pour cheese mixture onto biscuit base and bake for 1 hour and 10 minutes or until cooked (it will be slightly swollen, with a little colour). Cool in tin.

Carefully remove cheesecake from tin. To decorate, brush jam around the side of cheesecake and press on chopped pistachios. SERVES 8

Almond biscotti Delicious with coffee, these biscotti are also a great way to jazz up pannacotta. Alternatively, simply serve with a scoop of vanilla ice-cream and chocolate sauce.

3 egg whites

pinch of salt

180 g castor sugar

180 g plain flour, sifted

180 g blanched almonds

½ teaspoon ground cinnamon

Preheat oven to 180°C. Grease an 8 cm × 25 cm bar tin and line base with baking paper. Place egg whites and salt in the bowl of an electric mixer and beat until stiff peaks form. Gradually add sugar and beat for 30 seconds. Fold in flour, almonds and cinnamon.

Spoon mixture into the prepared tin and level with the back of a spoon. Bake for 30–40 minutes or until firm and cooked through. Remove from oven and allow to cool. Place in freezer for 1½ to 2 hours.

Preheat oven to 140°C. Line a baking tray with baking paper. Use a serrated knife to slice biscotti very thinly. Place biscotti on the tray and bake for 3–6 minutes or until very lightly brown and crisp. Allow to cool on tray. The biscotti can be stored for up to five days in an airtight container. MAKES ABOUT 50

Lemon and yoghurt cake with orange blossom salad

This is the easiest cake – simply blend all the ingredients together in a food processor. The orange blossom salad looks summery and tastes divine. For a change, try serving it with pavlova.

250 g soft unsalted butter

250 g castor sugar

4 eggs

1 lemon, zest finely grated

100 ml lemon juice

150 g plain yoghurt

⅓ cup (50 g) plain flour, sifted

250 g semolina

1⅔ cups (200 g) ground almonds

2 teaspoons baking powder

icing sugar, for dusting

200 g mascarpone, to serve

orange blossom salad

1 lemon, juiced

½ cup (110 g) castor sugar

1 teaspoon orange blossom water (see glossary)

2 mandarins, peeled and sliced

1 blood orange, peeled and segmented

1 large orange, peeled and segmented

1 lime, peeled and segmented

Preheat oven to 165°C. Grease a 26 cm round cake tin and line with baking paper. Blend butter and sugar in a food processor until pale and creamy. Add eggs, one at a time, pulsing after each addition. Add lemon zest, juice and yoghurt and process. Combine flour, semolina, ground almonds and baking powder. Add to butter mixture and process until smooth.

Spoon mixture into prepared tin and bake for 40–50 minutes or until cake is cooked when tested with a cake skewer. Turn onto a cake rack. When cool, dust with icing sugar. Serve with orange blossom salad and mascarpone.

To make orange blossom salad, place lemon juice, sugar and orange blossom water in a bowl. Add citrus segments and toss gently to combine. Set aside for 15 minutes, then serve. SERVES 8

Bitter chocolate torte
This torte is rich and fudgy. I can only eat a small piece with coffee but chocoholics will want a generous wedge with cream for dessert.

125 g butter, plus extra melted butter for greasing tin

435 g bitter dark chocolate, chopped,
    plus extra grated chocolate for lining tin

5 free-range eggs, separated

⅓ cup (80 ml) espresso coffee

100 ml brandy

130 g plain flour, sifted

pinch of salt

250 g castor sugar

bitter cocoa powder, for dusting

thick cream, to serve

Preheat oven to 165°C. Brush a 26 cm round spring-form cake tin with melted butter and line the base with baking paper. Coat sides of pan with grated chocolate.

Combine the remaining chocolate and butter in a bowl over a saucepan of simmering water (do not allow the bowl to touch the water). Stir until melted and smooth, then take off the heat and set aside to cool. Stir egg yolks into chocolate mixture one at a time, mixing well after each addition. Add coffee and brandy and stir. Add flour and mix until smooth.

Place egg whites in a large bowl with salt and beat until soft peaks form. Gradually pour in sugar and beat until thick and glossy. Gently fold egg whites into chocolate mixture in three batches, folding until mixture is smooth.

Pour mixture into prepared tin and bake for 1 hour or until top is crisp and a cake sewer comes out moist. Remove torte from oven and gently press down the edges. Turn oven off and return torte to oven for 1 hour to cool slowly. Allow torte to rest at room temperature for 30 minutes before unmoulding carefully.

To serve, dust with cocoa and serve with a dollop of cream. Do not refrigerate.

SERVES 8–10

Raspberries When raspberries are in season, I serve this chocolate torte at mr wolf with raspberries macerated in grappa and icing sugar.

Pinolate These biscuits should be soft and chewy in the middle with a delicate crust on the outside. The uncooked pinolate mixture keeps for up to three weeks in the fridge, so you can bake the biscuits fresh when friends drop in.

¾ cup (120 g) blanched almonds

570 g castor sugar

4 egg whites

⅔ cup (100 g) skinned, toasted hazelnuts

1⅔ cups (200 g) ground almonds

80 g butter

1 tablespoon honey

1 cup (150 g) pine nuts

1¼ cups (180 g) pistachios

icing sugar, for dusting

Place almonds, 270 g of the sugar and 3 of the egg whites in a food processor and blend until they form a smooth paste. Transfer mixture to a large bowl. Process remaining sugar, hazelnuts, ground almonds, butter, honey and remaining egg white in food processor until well combined. Combine almond and hazelnut mixtures, cover and place in the fridge for 1 hour.

Combine pine nuts and pistachios and chop coarsely.

Preheat oven to 150˚C. Line a baking tray with baking paper. Divide refrigerated mixture into small, oval balls the size of walnuts and roll in chopped pine nuts and pistachios to coat. Place on the tray and bake for 20 minutes or until pale gold. When cool, dust with icing sugar. Biscuits can be stored in an airtight container for up to four days. MAKES 50–60

Sweet treat For a quick sweet-tooth treat, try sesame brittle. Combine 85 g castor sugar, 250 g honey, 50 ml water and 2 pinches ground cinnamon in a heavy-based saucepan over low heat. Stir until sugar dissolves, then turn up heat to medium-high. Boil until 150°C on a sugar thermometer, or the syrup begins to darken. Add 125 g toasted blanched almonds and 375 g toasted sesame seeds. Remove from heat and stir gently. Pour onto a lightly oiled baking tray. When cool, break into chunks.

Glossary

These ingredients all have a place in my pantry or fridge, so that at the drop of a hat I can make any of my favourite dishes. They are not hard to find, and they can be used in so many different ways with such great results that I guarantee once you start experimenting with them in dishes you cook regularly, they will soon become almost household staples.

Baharat is a traditional Turkish spice blend that combines pepper with any or all of the following: paprika, cumin, coriander, cinnamon, cloves, cardamom, star anise and nutmeg. It is available from supermarkets and Middle-Eastern shops.

Banana capsicums are mild-flavoured, yellow–green capsicums in the shape of over-grown chillis.

Burghul is cracked wheat and comes in many grades, from fine to coarse. The wheat is boiled, then dried and ground to become burghul. It is available from supermarkets and Middle-Eastern shops.

Cavolo nero grows in long dark green stalks and can be picked very young and eaten raw in well-dressed salads, or picked later and cooked as a vegetable. It has a cabbage-like flavour and is also known as Tuscan kale.

Fontina is a semi-soft cow's milk cheese with a sweet delicate flavour. Along with Parmesan, it is one of the best cooking or melting cheeses.

Fromage frais and goat's curd are cheeses made from fresh, uncooked and unsalted curd. They have a short shelf-life, but their unique flavour and texture cannot be replaced with a cooked milk cheese.

Gelatine is a neutral material used to 'set' foods. Available in powder and sheet form (I only use sheets), gelatine comes in varying strengths, graded as bronze, silver and gold. I use Alba gold leaf or Gelita gold leaf (both weigh 10 g for 6 sheets).

Goat's curd *see* fromage frais

Gorgonzola is a cow's-milk blue-veined cheese named after its place of origin, an area that is now part of the eastern suburbs of Milan. The veins are formed by pricking the cheese with long needles to expose the interior, which enables mould to form. Gorgonzola Piccante is an aged version that is slightly sharper and more intense than the younger cheese, Gorgonzola Dolce.

Harissa in its simplest form, which is found almost all over North Africa, is a firey paste made from reconstituted dried chillies mixed with tomato paste and salt. More complex recipes include other spices, and green harissa is made with green chillies. (See my recipe for fresh harissa on page 194.)

Iranian couscous is larger than regular, fine couscous, and approximately half the size of the pea-size couscous called Maghreb found throughout Lebanon. Iranian couscous has the slippery texture of pasta when cooked, and a toasted version is commonly sold in Jewish supermarkets.

Kefalograviera is a hard cheese made from goat's or sheep's milk. It has a tangy flavour and is often grated, grilled, or cut into thin triangles and fried.

Orange blossom water is water that has been infused with an extract of the blossom of orange trees. A heady, intense liquid commonly used in salads and desserts and refreshing in cold lemon drinks and teas, it is available from specialist food stores and Middle-Eastern and Greek delis.

Palm sugar, also known as jaggery, is a sugar obtained from the sap of palm trees. I buy mine in a light-to-dark-brown block and grate it, as required, using the coarse side of a grater.

Pancetta is an Italian-style bacon. It is salt-cured pork belly, rolled tightly or curved flat, and sometimes spiced with dry chilli. Quality pancetta can be eaten like salami, sliced thickly for braises or thinly sliced and grilled to be eaten crisp in salads and soups.

Pecorino is a hard sheep's-milk cheese (although cow's milk is sometimes added), produced in central and southern Italy. There are several different types of Pecorino, each with a regional accent. I use Pecorino Romano in my recipes.

Pomegranate molasses is concentrated pomegranate juice that has been reduced very slowly to create a sweet–sour syrup used sparingly in dressings and marinades. It should have a honey-like consistency. The brand I prefer is AL-RABIH. It is available from specialist and Middle-Eastern shops.

Pomegranate seeds have a fruity sweet flavour and a tart pip. Use them fresh in salads and desserts. To extract them, take a fresh pomegranate and cut through the red, leathery skin to the honeycomb pith, where you will find red jewel-like glassy seeds. Scoop these out with a spoon and remove the pith and membranes.

Ras el hanout is a very special blend of spices – the name means 'spice of the house'. The recipe is usually a spice vendor's secret and may include up to thirty spices or more. A humble blend may consist of cumin, coriander, cardamom, sweet paprika, turmeric, cayenne powder, sugar, allspice and cinnamon. It is available from specialist and Middle-Eastern shops.

Red basil is a variety of the more common sweet basil. It tastes the same as sweet basil, but its ruby coloured leaves look particularly good in salads.

Sumac is a powder ground from a sharp-tasting Middle-Eastern berry. Sumac should always have a deep burgundy colour, and is available from spice shops, delis and supermarkets.

Taleggio is a soft cow's milk cheese. It is high in fat, has a reddish soft rind and a sweet buttery texture, and is one of Italy's most famous cheeses. Taleggio is a popular table cheese and is also excellent for cooking.

Tahini is a smooth paste made from ground white sesame seeds, with a little salt added. It is very intense, has a high oil content and will go rancid after it has been open for a couple of months. Keep it refrigerated.

Tamari is a naturally fermented soy sauce made from soybeans and without any wheat. It is usually darker in colour than the more common soy sauce.

Verjuice is made from unripened grapes, usually semillon or chardonnay. It has a more mellow flavour than lemon juice or wine vinegar but can be used in place of these ingredients. It is available from delis and gourmet food stores.

Vincotto is a type of vinegar. This thick syrup, traditionally made in southern Italy, is made by cooking the must (the unfermented juice from grapes that have been pressed to make wine), until the liquid is the consistency of honey. It is used as a condiment in dressings and drizzled over sweet and savoury food just before serving. It is available from Italian and specialist food stores.

References

Arabesque Lucy and Greg Malouf (Hardie Grant, Melbourne 2002)

The Cook's Companion Stephanie Alexander (Lantern, Melbourne 2004)

The Gastronomy of Italy Anna Del Conte (Pavilion Books, London 2004)

The Oxford Companion to Food Alan Davidson (Oxford University Press, Oxford 1999)

Acknowledgements

This book would have been just recipes and photographs with a few simple introductions if not for the help of good friend and talented writer Marcus Ellis, who turned my clumsy words into proper book and chapter introductions that are both entertaining and heartfelt. Marcus, thank you also for your fine palate and intellectual creativity – your honesty and input have been supportive in so many different ways over the last ten years xx.

There are many other people who have helped me with this book in both practical and subtle ways . . .

My family and friends have always been there for me in every way, including giving my new recipes a try; accepting last-minute dinner invitations to our house at odd hours; and throwing open the doors of their own houses for me to come and make a mess and a feast (celebrating both the successful and the not so successful – happily there weren't too many of those!) Thank you to Emma and Damien, Daniel and Alona, Simon and Lea, Craig and Leigh and Jacqueline, Ben and Charlotte, Leanne and Tim. Thanks to my fellow chef Paul, for your professional and personal support and enthusiasm. Thank you to Lindy and Marty, who were so welcoming when I was the new kid on the block. Your friendship and constant encouragement are treasured – as are all the late-night Longrain memories.

A big loving thank you to my ever-adoring parents, Monica and Pierre, who have offered me so much love, and who encouraged me from such a tender young age to follow my heart and to succeed in whatever I chose to do. Also to my Meme, for her patience in guiding me slowly through the Tunisian family recipes, and for passing on those strong good-cooking genes and teaching me that love is a really important ingredient in any recipe.

To my sisters, Justine and Odette, for their love and constant support for their older sister, who, in the past, rarely returned phone calls promptly and missed the occasional birthday due to the crazy demands of the hospitality business.

To my cousin Simone, who is always looking out for me and whose guidance and words of wisdom have been with me always.

To Petrina, it is always a pleasure. Thank you for your compliments and advice, and for the beautiful photographs of my food, which have given so much life and beauty to this book. A big thank you to Emma Knowles, who did the amazing styling in nearly all the photographs – your faffing was never too much.

Many thanks to Lisa Hudson, for having the vision and giving me the opportunity to share my recipes with many through *Sunday Life* magazine; and to Kirsten and her professional team at *Sunday Life*. Thank you also to Lynn, for testing all my (sometimes loosely written) recipes and making them perfect for everyone.

A massive thank you to Julie Gibbs, for giving me a chance to shine and publish with Lantern at Penguin. Her constant support and calming words of wisdom are cherished. Thanks also to Deborah and Susan and the extremely efficient team at Penguin, for pulling this book together in such a crazy timeframe.

A special thanks to Marika, Marissa, Kylie and Tascha and all my staff, front and back of house, for their support and enthusiasm through all my busy times.

To Marino Angelini, friend and business partner, and Rosa, his lovely wife, thank you for your constant support and guidance, and love and good wishes over the last ten years.

Mr Craig Andrade, your professional advice, support and generous enthusiasm have been overwhelming and are most appreciated – thanks.

Jacinta, Kevin and Julie and everyone at creative\token – what would I do without you all? You're a fantastic team; it has been a roller-coaster ride over the last six months and I feel very comfortable being in your professional hands. Thanks for getting all my ducks in a straight line.

To my honey, Michael, thank you for your love, passion, strength, creativity, never-ending encouragement and patience. May you always have an appetite for my cooking . . . and me.

Index

LANTERN

Published by the Penguin Group
Penguin Group (Australia)
250 Camberwell Road, Camberwell, Victoria 3124, Australia
(a division of Pearson Australia Group Pty Ltd)
Penguin Group (USA) Inc.
375 Hudson Street, New York, New York 10014, USA
Penguin Group (Canada)
90 Eglinton Avenue East, Suite 700, Toronto ON M4P 2Y3, Canada
(a division of Pearson Penguin Canada Inc.)
Penguin Books Ltd
80 Strand, London WC2R 0RL, England
Penguin Ireland
25 St Stephen's Green, Dublin 2, Ireland
(a division of Penguin Books Ltd)
Penguin Books India Pvt Ltd
11 Community Centre, Panchsheel Park, New Delhi – 110 017, India
Penguin Group (NZ)
Cnr Airborne and Rosedale Roads, Albany, Auckland, New Zealand
(a division of Pearson New Zealand Ltd)
Penguin Books (South Africa) (Pty) Ltd
24 Sturdee Avenue, Rosebank, Johannesburg 2196, South Africa

Penguin Books Ltd, Registered Offices:
80 Strand, London WC2R 0RL, England

First published by Penguin Group (Australia), 2006

10 9 8 7 6 5 4 3 2 1

Text copyright © Karen Martini 2006
Photographs copyright © Petrina Tinslay 2006

The moral right of the author has been asserted

Cover and text design by Nikki Townsend © Penguin Group (Australia)
Photography by Petrina Tinslay
Food stylist Emma Knowles; food styling on pages 6, 11, 77, 100, 117, 185 and 195 by Yael Grinham
Typeset in Minion and Antique Olive by Post Pre-press Group, Brisbane, Queensland
Colour reproduction by Splitting Image Colour Studio Pty Ltd, Clayton, Victoria
Printed and bound in China by 1010 Printing International Limited

National Library of Australia
Cataloguing-in-Publication data:

Martini, Karen.
Karen martini where the heart is.
Includes index.
ISBN-13: 978 1 920989 52 1.
ISBN-10: 1 920989 52 8.
1. Cookery.   I. Title.

641.5

www.penguin.com.au

Photos: back cover photo, Dark chocolate mousse (p213);
opposite title page, Corella pear, pecorino, walnut and currant salad (p26);
opposite contents page, Champagne jelly with grapes, ricotta and crushed amaretti (p203);
ingredients page, Pizza no. 9 at mr wolf (p16)